VALUES

Suggested Activities to
Motivate the Teaching of
Values Clarification

AUTHOR
WILLIAM HENDRICKS

Published by
EDUCATIONAL SERVICE, INC.
P.O. Box 219
Stevensville, Michigan 49127

Copyright 1984©
EDUCATIONAL SERVICE, INC.
P.O. Box 219
Stevensville, Michigan 49127
Printed in the U.S.A.
ISBN #89273-137-0

TABLE OF CONTENTS

PAGE
SECTION ONE: VALUES RELATED TO ONE'S PERSON

Chapter One: "Values That are Chiefly Unseen or Internal"
1. What a Long Time to Wait!......2
2. Scars......3
3. Solving Shyness......4
4. How Are They Different?......6
5. Dealing With Your Feelings......6
6. Are You a Puppet?......8
7. You Decide......9
8. All About Me......10
9. You Can Choose Only One......11
10. These Are a Few of Our Favorite Things......12
11. Mirror, Mirror on the Wall......14
12. Passive or Agressive......15
13. I Meant To Do My Work Today......16
14. I'm Glad I'm Not a Tree......17
15. The Sun Is Always Shining......18
16. Changing Faces......19
17. I Wish......20
18. Honesty Haiku......21
19. Examine the Consequences or Results......22
20. Value Center......23
21. Do Clothes Make the Person?......25
22. How Much TV?......26
23. Personal Preferences......27
24. Accepting Praise Graciously......28
25. Fingerprints......30

Chapter Two: "Values That Are More External and Are Often Expressed in Words and Actions"

1. Look At the Bright Side......33

2. Good Manners Morning........................34
3. Let's Put Fruit on the Helpfulness Tree..........35
4. What Is Leadership?............................36
5. Help Wanted......................................37
6. Like Dominos....................................38
7. Serve As a Travel Consultant....................39
8. Analyzing Inconsistencies........................40
9. Planning Your Time.............................41
10. Courtesy Mobiles................................43
11. Choosing a Pet..................................44
12. A Four Way Test.................................45
13. A Timely Topic..................................46
14. Who Do You Trust?..............................47
15. Lost and Found..................................48
16. Agreeable or Disagreeable.......................49
17. A Contest..50

SECTION TWO: VALUES RELATED TO THE FAMILY

1. My Family Is Where I Belong...................53
2. What Parents Do For Us.........................53
3. Send a Card......................................54
4. Helping At Home.................................55
5. Where Have You Been?..........................57
6. Roots..58
7. Pleasantness In Unpleasantness..................59
8. Housekeeping Corner............................60
9. Task Choices.....................................61
10. Table Talk Topics................................62
11. Family Members Bill of Rights...................63
12. Caring For Family Property......................64
13. Comic Strips Speak..............................65
14. Showing Love....................................66

SECTION THREE: VALUES RELATED TO OUR HUMAN RELATIONSHIPS

1. The Blind Men and the Elephant................69

2. Winners Or Losers 70
  3. Appreciation Time 70
  4. Let's Play Ann Landers 72
  5. Employer-Employee Relationships 73
  6. I'm a Member 74
  7. Cattlemen vs. Sheepherders 75
  8. Little People 76
  9. Because 77
 10. Shadows 79
 11. Potlatch 80
 12. Consider Robin Hood 81
 13. Helpers Club 82
 14. War Or Peace 83
 15. What's In a Name? 84
 16. Choices Between Opposites 85
 17. Don't Embarrass Others 86
 18. Say Something Nice 87
 19. Compliment Time 88
 20. Persons Or Objects 89
 21. No Man Is An Island 90
 22. Things Done By and For Others 90
 23. Shared Interest Groups 92
 24. Making Introductions 93
 25. Telephone Manners 93

SECTION FOUR: VALUES RELATED TO PERSONAL HEALTH

  1. Should I Smoke? 96
  2. Good Or Bad? 97
  3. Cleanliness Chart 98
  4. Growth Folder 99
  5. Helen Keller's Lesson 100
  6. Health Servant's Collage 100
  7. Just Suppose 102
  8. Is It Just Good Or Good For You? 103
  9. Traits Or Habits 103
 10. To Love Your Work 105

11. Working Through One's Hostile Feelings.........106
12. How Do You Feel Today? 107
13. Rites of Passage.............................108

SECTION FIVE: VALUES RELATED TO AUTHORITY AND GOVERNMENT

1. Would You Ride With Paul Revere? 112
2. Overtime Parking..............................113
3. Like the Pieces of a Jigsaw Puzzle 114
4. Is Freedom of Speech Really Free?.............116
5. Righting Wrongs..............................116
6. Preamble Study...............................117
7. A Pledge Is a Promise 119
8. When Others Are Watching 120
9. Is It Fit To Eat? 121
10. Penalties For Drug Abuse 123
11. What Is a Law?...............................124
12. Make a Graph 125
13. On Trial......................................125
14. Not Like Lightning 126
15. Right, Wrong Or Maybe 127
16. Campaign Promises 128
17. Simulating Signing the Declaration of Independence.129
18. Who Made the Rules? 130

SECTION SIX: VALUES RELATED TO PROPERTY

1. For Sale 133
2. If I Had a Million Dollars 134
3. Put It In the Bank 135
4. Analyzing Advertising 136
5. A Broken Window.............................137
6. Spray Paint 138
7. Finders Keepers................................139

8. Choosing the Right Tool 140
9. Workaholics 141
10. When You Borrow Something 142
11. What Can I Do With Money? 144
12. Wise Consumers 145
13. Who Owns It? 146
14. Private Property--Keep Out 147
15. Needs Or Wants? 148
16. Returning a Few Pennies 149
17. Handle It Gently 150
18. Learning to Fish 151

SECTION SEVEN: VALUES RELATED TO EDUCATION

1. Homework First 154
2. Library Book Returns 155
3. Is Your Desk Well-Organized? 156
4. Why Study This? 157
5. When Others Make Mistakes 158
6. Cheating On a Test 159
7. It's Raining 160
8. Sifting Facts From Opinions 161
9. Fact Or Fiction 162
10. For Or Against 163
11. Learning Contracts 165
12. Math Skills Applied 166
13. Success Record 166
14. Exercising Self-Discipline 167
15. Tattle Tale 168
16. Welcoming Committee 170
17. Desk Name Card 170
18. Number Line 172
19. Use It Together 173

SECTION EIGHT: VALUES RELATED TO CULTURE

1. What If We Had No Music 175
2. The First Thanksgiving 176
3. Historical Amnesia 178
4. Where Did We Get Our Customs? 179
5. Using Scientific Knowledge 180
6. Who Produced It? 181
7. Family Heirlooms 183
8. Heroes In History 183
9. Song Analysis 184
10. Library Book Character Day 185
11. Time Capsule 186
12. Language Differences 187
13. Renaissance Art 188
14. Handicaps of Great People 190
15. Without Prejudice 191
16. Christmas Customs 192
17. Starting a New Colony 193
18. Visiting the Symphony 194

SECTION NINE: VALUES RELATED TO ENVIRONMENT

1. Turn Off That Unused Light 197
2. Avoid Accidents 198
3. Wash Out 199
4. Don't Be a Litterbug 201
5. Write Your Own Picture Caption 203
6. Always In Their Own Orbit 204
7. Extinct 205
8. Our Orderly Seasons 206
9. Who Needs Water? 207
10. Wasting Water 208
11. You Can't Live Without It 209
12. A Park Or a Parking Lot 210
13. Mineral Deposits 211
14. Collect and Recycle 211
15. Prevent Forest Fires 212

16. When the Electricity Is Off....................213
17. Keep Off the Grass--Don't Pick the Flowers.....214
18. Ground Hog Day.............................215
19. Arbor Day..................................216
20. Noise Pollution.............................217
21. When a Tree Burns..........................218

SECTION ONE

VALUES RELATED TO ONE'S PERSON

The activities suggested in this section are designed to help students develop those personal values necessary for happy and worthwhile lives. Chapter One includes values that are chiefly unseen or internal while those in Chapter Two are more external and are often expressed in words or actions.

Chapter One

Values that are chiefly unseen or internal.

1. WHAT A LONG TIME TO WAIT!
(Grades 1-5)
VALUE: PATIENCE

A. Purpose: To provide opportunity for pupils to understand and practice patience.

B. Materials: A calendar showing holidays and other special occasions that are important to the children in your class.

C. Procedure: Hang up a large wall calendar that has all of the months of the year on it. Ask the pupils to name their favorite holidays. As they respond, circle the date; for example, if the child says Christmas is his/her favorite holiday, circle December 25.

Next, ask the pupils to name their favorite sport. Try to determine with the class when a seasonal sport ends; for example, baseball ends with the *World Series* in October, sledding ends when the snow melts. Circle the ending dates of these favorite seasons.

After several dates have been circled on your calendar, move to a discussion of the idea of waiting and of patience. Use the following questions as discussion starters:

1. How do you feel the day after Christmas when you suddenly realize that next Christmas is a whole year away?

2. How do you feel when you put your sled away in the spring, knowing that you will not be able to use it again until next winter?

3. Does it help to be impatient?

4. Does being impatient make us unhappy?

D. Variation: Whenever a child gives evidence of being unusually impatient or the total class reflects the need to grow in the ability to be patient, discuss the topic openly. Have the class suggest ways in which adults must "wait." Use the following examples to start the discussion:

    a. How does a farmer who plants a crop or an orchard exercise patience?

    b. How does a driver at a red light or on a highway when a flagman stops traffic because of construction exercise patience? What might happen if the driver didn't?

Conclude the lesson by having pupils suggest ways in which being properly patient can bring happiness and being unduly impatient can bring unhappiness.

2. SCARS (Grades 4-7)
VALUE: SELF-ACCEPTANCE

A. Purpose: To help pupils accept scars they may have received through accidents as well as understand how to treat peers who have scars.

B. Materials: Information about scar tissue; how it is formed and why it is important.

C. Procedure: Note with your class that nearly everyone has had accidents of one kind or another that have caused scars.

Discuss the miraculous process of skin growth and the way that cuts, scratches, and even severe wounds are closed through healing in a very few days or weeks.

Note that scars are not painful, that they tend to grow less obvious as a person grows older, and that they stand for something that is now past.

Should we worry about scars? No.

Should we worry about what people think when they see scars we may have? No.

Should we ridicule people who have scars? No.

Instead we should be thankful for the healing that caused the scars.

Scars often tell the story of self-sacrifice. For example, a father might have scars on his hands if he saved his child from a fire; a policeman or fireman might have scars from injuries he received while helping others; a soldier, sailor or marine may have the scar of a wound received while he was fighting for his country or the nail scars in Jesus's hands and feet show that he died on the cross to save others. Some of the class members may have scars because of injuries received while helping others also.

D. Variation: To make pupils less self-conscious about any scars they have, you may wish to give them the opportunity to show their scars and tell how they were received.

3. SOLVING SHYNESS (Grades 3-6)
VALUE: SELF-CONFIDENCE

A. Purpose: To help pupils understand what shyness is and how to overcome it.

B. Materials: Information about a "case study" situation so that pupils can play the role of advisors.

C. Procedure: Have half of the class imagine that they are one of the following students:

Student 1: This student is approximately ten years old. She is withdrawn and shy. She gets average grades in school but could do better if she could enter into discussions and make reports more freely. She is doing well in her piano lessons which she takes outside of school hours.

Student 2: This student is also approximately 10 years old. He is muscular and well-coordinated but lacks confidence in his skill. If he makes a mistake while playing a game, he feels shy and tries to avoid meeting his teammates after the game. In school his work is just below average.

Student 3: This student comes from a poor family and is generally dressed "differently" from the other children because she must wear "hand-me-down" clothes from older sisters or cousins. She does excellent work in her academic subjects but withdraws from participating with the other students in outside-of-class activities.

Have the other half of the class imagine that they are the school counsellors so that the class is divided into pairs, one the student, the other the counsellor.

Ask the "student" and the "counsellor" to discuss the student's problem and try to arrive at some solutions to help the student increase his/her self-confidence.

After a given period of time, such as five or ten minutes, have the pupils exchange roles and partners and repeat the discussion.

Summarize the discussion by having the pupils share with the total class the best ideas they were able to formulate to overcome shyness and develop self-confidence.

D. Variation: After discussing one or all of the "case studies" suggested, have the class write descriptions of similar problems and feelings related to shyness and self-confidence that they have experienced. Have the class discuss these problems and share solutions.

4. HOW ARE THEY DIFFERENT? (Grades K-4)
VALUE: PERSONAL DIGNITY

A. Purpose: To strengthen the sense of personal dignity of students by emphasizing the difference between human beings and animals.

B. Materials: Bulletin board space. A variety of pictures of animals and people.

C. Procedure: Mount the following caption on your bulletin board:

HOW ARE THEY DIFFERENT?
PERSONS   ANIMALS

Have pupils comment and mount a wide variety of pictures of both animals and persons engaged in a wide range of activities. After a sizeable collection has been assembled, hold a discussion based on a comparison of the activities of which animals and human beings are capable.

Conclude the lesson by having the pupils write a story or theme using the heading, "Because I'm a Person."

5. DEALING WITH YOUR FEELINGS (Grades 5-8)
VALUE: STABILITY

A. Purpose: To help pupils realize that every person experiences a wide range of feelings and that we must deal with them in socially acceptable and stable ways.

B. Materials: Chart paper, felt pen and 3 x 5 inch cards.

C. Procedure: Discuss the various feelings people experience. Ask how students feel under the following circumstances:

1. Your school basketball team is tied with the

team of another school during a championship game and there are just two minutes left to play. You have the ball for the last shot, the ball is in the air and you miss.

2. The teacher announces that you have the only perfect paper in the class on a hard test.

3. You drop your tray, with your noon lunch, with a loud clatter in the school cafeteria and your friends laugh at you.

Add other unusual situations that arouse strong feelings from the real-life experience of the pupils in your class.

Make a list of the various circumstances or situations on the chart paper with your felt pen.

Distribute the 3 x 5 inch cards and ask the pupils to write how they would feel if one of the situations happened to them. Then they should write an acceptable response on one side and an unacceptable response on the other side.

Divide the class into groups of 3-5 pupils and have them discuss the responses suggested. Then have each group select the best response and share it with the class. Conclude the discussion with an emphasis on the importance of stability when responding to situations in which high levels of personal feelings are involved.

D. Variation: Bring a few newspaper articles about social or political situations that reflect strong feelings on the part of the persons who are involved in the situation. Show these to the class and use them to illustrate the difference between persons who do and those who do not control themselves in stable ways. Discuss how the citizens of a country depend on the stability of their leaders and how we all depend on the stability of one another.

6. ARE YOU A PUPPET? (Grades 4-7)
VALUE: SELF-CONTROL

A. Purpose: To help pupils realize that persons who are addicted to any substance have lost part of their self-control.

B. Materials: Puppets for a puppet play. These could be either the finger or "hand-inside" type or the more complex type that are manipulated by strings.

C. Procedure: Explain how puppets are made and manipulated at a puppet show. Demonstrate those you have by making them say and do things for the class to observe. Use the following questions to stimulate a discussion on self-control:

1. What makes the puppet move?
2. Does the puppet think for itself?
3. How are people different from puppets?
4. What happens to a person if he/she takes drugs or alcohol that cause a person to lose his/her self-control?
5. In what way is a person who lets someone else do the thinking for him something like a puppet?
6. Is a person who says and does things while under the influence of drugs or alcohol that he would never do otherwise something like a puppet?

Conclude the discussion by pointing out how important it is for us to exercise self-control in all the things we say and do.

Select a story from one of their reading lessons or a favorite fairy tale and have them make the characters as puppets. After the play is over have pupils note how the puppets were made to say words over which they had no self-control and to make movements for which they were not responsible.

Compare this to what happens to a person who turns the controls of his nervous system over to drugs or alcohol.

7. YOU DECIDE (Grades K-4)
VALUE: RESPONSIBILITY

A. Purpose: To help pupils develop a sense of personal responsibility for their own health and well-being.

B. Materials: Chart paper, felt pen.

C. Procedure: Introduce the idea of "deciding" to your class by talking about the many things in one's daily life about which decisions must be made. Include the idea that some of these decisions are made for us; such as if our parents call us to get up in the morning. Some we make for ourselves; such as if we decide when to get up, set the alarm clock and get up by ourselves.

Using chart paper and a felt pen, make a chart form similar to that shown below:

Decisions of Ages 1-3	Made By
Decisions of Ages 4-6	Made By
Decisions of Ages 7-9	Made By

As pupils make suggestions, fill in the chart with your felt pen. Note with them how many decisions were made for you by others when you were very young, and how, as you grew older, you began making more decisions for yourself. Use the following questions to continue the discussion:

1. What kinds of things do you need to assume responsibility for now? (Solicit answers such as dressing warmly in cold weather; choosing nourishing food, avoiding the use of substances that are harmful to the body, etc.)

2. Why can **only you** make and carry out these decisions? (Parents and teachers cannot always be with you, etc.)

D. Variation: Have pupils make a list of decisions that are difficult for them. Hold a discussion on how wise decisions are made. Include the following steps:

1. Defining the problem or issue clearly.
2. Gathering the needed information to make the decision knowledgeably.
3. Consider all possible results and appropriate alternatives.
4. Choose the best response.
5. Carry out the decision in action.

8. ALL ABOUT ME (Grades K-3)
VALUE: SELF-IDENTITY

A. Purpose: To help pupils strengthen their sense of self-identity by assembling a collage of pictures related to their personal interests.

B. Materials: A number of magazines from which pictures can be freely cut. Scissors, glue and poster paper.

C. Procedure: Print the words "ALL ABOUT ME" on the chalkboard and introduce the lesson by calling to mind ways in which we are all different. Use the following questions to help pupils develop their sense of self-identity:

    1. What are some of your favorite foods?
    2. What are some of your favorite sports or games?
    3. What do you hope to be when you grow up?
    4. What is your favorite subject in school?

Add questions about such items as your favorite color, your favorite item of clothing, etc.

Next distribute the poster paper and have pupils print the caption, ALL ABOUT ME, on it. Using the old magazines and scissors, have the pupils look for and cut out pictures of items they listed in response to the questions about themselves.

Pupils should glue the pictures they cut out to the poster paper to make a collage that depicts some of their personal interests. Allow each child to display the collage he/she has made and explain it to the class.

9. YOU CAN ONLY CHOOSE ONE (Grades 5-8) VALUE: WISE JUDGMENT

A. Purpose: To help pupils realize the importance of wise choices.

B. Materials: A copy of the poem "The Road Not Taken" by Robert Frost. Chalkboard.

C. Procedure: Begin by discussing the many situations in life when everyone must make choices. Point out that many times choosing one thing often eliminates other things, for example:

    1. If we choose between doing our homework or going out to play, our choice to do one makes it

impossible, for that moment at least, to do the other.

   2. If we choose between going away or staying home, by choosing one we eliminate the other.

   3. If we choose between going east or west, by going one way, we decide not to go the other.

Have pupils suggest other "choices" that illustrate how choosing for one thing may force you automatically to choose against something else.

Read the poem, "The Road Not Taken" by Robert Frost to your class. Then draw a picture of a road on the chalkboard. Make the road with a Y or "fork" in it and explain how the traveler who comes to the Y must choose to go down one way or the other.

Robert Frost puts into beautiful poetic language the problem of the traveler. He emphasizes how difficult it is for someone who chooses to start down one way to return and go down the other road as well.

Ask pupils if they can think of times in their lives when they had to make decisions between two such "roads" and why the choices they made were difficult to reverse. Help pupils to understand and appreciate that the choices they make each day have many important long-range consequences. Encourage them to use wise judgment in making their choices.

10. THESE ARE A FEW OF OUR FAVORITE THINGS (Grades K-4)
VALUE: PERSONAL PREFERENCES

   A. Purpose: To help pupils realize that each person has his/her own preferences, that these may be different from the preferences of others and that we should respect these differences.

B. Materials: A somewhat secluded corner of the classroom that has a bulletin board and a table.

C. Procedure: Mount the following caption on the bulletin board, "THESE ARE A FEW OF MY FAVORITE THINGS." Introduce the idea of the individual differences we all have in the things we like best. During the first week, have pupils cut out a picture from a magazine at home of a favorite food. Ask them to mount the picture with their name on the bulletin board. During the next week have them bring a favorite toy to place on the table. Be sure each item is clearly identified. Another item that could be included would be a favorite book, their favorite song (perhaps writing the title and their name on a 3 x 5 inch card and mounting it on the bulletin board) a favorite sport, team, etc.

Allow pupils to browse in the corner during some free time to note the different choices of others and the favorite things of other class members.

You should provide some time and opportunity throughout the project for pupils to explain to others what they like about their favorite things.

Conclude the learning activity with a discussion about individual differences. Note not only the wide range of things we like and are interested in, but also what a wide range of differences there is among ourselves in size, ability, appearance, etc. Just as we respect the right that a person has to like something different from us, so we must respect each other person for being different as well.

11. MIRROR, MIRROR ON THE WALL
(Grades K-1)
VALUE: SELF-IDENTITY

A. Purpose: To strengthen the pupils' sense of self-identity.

B. Materials: A full-length (for children) mirror.

C. Procedure: Mount the mirror at some place in the classroom where it is not easily damaged yet where it is readily accessible to the children.

Plan one activity per week that would require each pupil to view himself/herself in the mirror. Examples might include:

    1. After removing your caps and before you go to your seats, check your appearance in the mirror and "smooth down" your hair.

    2. After you have your coats, caps, etc., on, check yourself in the mirror to be sure all buttons and zippers are tied or closed properly.

    3. Practice a smile — wear it all day.

    4. Hold up your hands to the mirror to check for cleanliness.

    5. Stand with a child before the mirror occasionally and note how he/she has grown.

    6. Stand with a child before the mirror occasionally if a shoelace is loose and have him/her notice and correct the problem.

    7. Stand with a child before the mirror to note how nice the pupil looks in her new hair ribbon or his new coat.

By using the mirror regularly in an informal and natural way, the teacher can strengthen the child's sense of self-identity in a wholesome on-going way.

D. Variation: Make a duplicated sheet similar to the one that follows:

> My name is _____.
>
> I have _____ hair.
>   (color)
>
> I have _____ eyes.
>   (color)
>
> My favorite color is _____.
>
> My favorite sport is _____.
>
> My favorite book is _____.
>
> (Add other personal interests of your pupils.)

Have the pupils check items two and three in the classroom mirror before completing the blanks. Conclude the exercise by noting how we are all different and how happy we may be that we are ourselves.

12. PASSIVE OR AGGRESSIVE? (Grades 6-8)
VALUE: SELF-CONTROL

A. Purpose: To help pupils react in controlled ways when others act offensively toward them.

B. Materials: Two large sheets of poster paper. Felt pen.

C. Procedure: Write the terms, "ACTIVE" on one sheet of poster paper and "PASSIVE" on the other. Show them to the class and then explain the terms.

Next have pupils listen to or role play the following situation: One student is working at her desk when another pushes against her roughly. Classify the following possible responses as either passive or active:

1. Ignore the disturbance.
2. Criticize the offender; tell the person how clumsy he/she is.
3. Move to another desk.
4. Shout at the person who pushed you.
5. Push the offender back at least as hard or harder than you were pushed.
6. Tell the person you are sorry your chair was in his/her way.

As the students classify and agree upon the classification of the response, use your felt pen to write them on the appropriate poster.

Next discuss the two ways, active or passive, to respond to offensive behavior of others.

Point out how hard it sometimes is to react calmly and passively when others are aggressive against you.

D. Variation: Instead of using this learning activity as a large group or total class lesson, use it with an individual child or a few children who have had a quarrel that involves aggressive behavior.

13. I MEANT TO DO MY WORK TODAY
(Grades 4-7)
VALUE: KEEPING WORK AND ENJOYMENT IN BALANCE

A. Purpose: To help pupils realize that work is important but needs to be kept in balance with enjoyment and relaxation.

B. Materials: A copy of the poem, "I Meant To Do My Work Today" by Richard LeGallienne which can be found in many anthologies of children's poetry.

C. Procedure: Begin the lesson by talking about the need to work and earn a living. Use the following questions as discussion starters:

1. How much time do we spend working each day?
2. What frame of mind must we have to do our work well?
3. What does it mean to be a "workaholic"?

Next read the poem, "I Meant To Do My Work Today" by Richard LeGallienne to the class.

Discuss the way the person in the poem felt when he heard the bird singing in the apple tree, saw the butterfly, etc.

Summarize the lesson by discussing the need to keep a healthy balance between the time we spend working and the need for times of enjoyment and relaxation.

14. I'M GLAD I'M NOT A TREE (Grades K-3)
VALUE: MOBILITY

A. Purpose: To help pupils appreciate their ability to move.

B. Materials: A picture of a crowd of people and a grove of trees.

C. Procedure: Show your class a picture of a crowd of people and a grove of trees. Ask them to name as many differences between the crowd of people and the grove of trees as possible.

Move the focus from the discussion of several differences to the consideration of the quality of mobility which people possess.

Ask the pupils to imagine what life would be like if they could not move about but would have to remain in one place like a tree. After discussing the ideas suggested by the pupils, have them develop their wonder and appreciation for their ability to move by acting for a short time as if they were "rooted" to one place.

Conclude the activity by having the pupils express their appreciation for their mobility by telling, writing or drawing their reactions to the experience of acting as though they were immobile.

15. THE SUN IS ALWAYS SHINING (Grades 3-6) VALUE: OPTIMISM

A. Purpose: To help pupils develop a sense of optimism in times of trouble and difficulty.

B. Materials: A picture of rain clouds with the sun shining through at various openings.

C. Procedure: Show pupils a picture of the sun shining far above the earth with a small layer of clouds near the earth and perhaps a rain shower falling.

Note with your class how the clouds may separate the earth from the sun without the sun even seeming to notice them at all.

Then compare the natural sunshine to happy times in our lives. Point out to the class that just as there may be times when rain clouds tend to separate us from the sunshine, so we have times of unhappiness and trouble.

Hold a class discussion about the attitudes people have toward the troubles and unhappy events in their lives. Use the following questions as discussion starters:

    1. What kinds of good things can you do to

fill your time when you are sick?

2. How can some people who have severe handicaps or long-term illnesses be so cheerful?

3. What is the best way to react at the time of illness and sorrow in your life or in the lives of your friends?

Remind them that we can be optimistic because just as the rain clouds often break apart and allow the sunshine through so the troubles and problems in our lives will often allow rays of joy and happiness to shine through as well.

D. Variation: Discuss ways in which members of your class can add some cheer to the life of some "shut-in" in your community.

16. CHANGING FACES (Grades 3-6)
VALUE: CONSISTENCY

A. Purpose: To help pupils realize that we all have many "faces" and to encourage them to wear a happy expression.

B. Materials: Science textbooks or other library materials that show the different phases the moon has during the time of a 28 day cycle. Paper and pencils. A calendar showing the moon's phases for the current month.

C. Procedure: On a morning after the moon had been particularly clear the night before, ask how many children had seen it. Have a few children describe its shape. Introduce the concept of the changing phases of the moon by showing pictures of the various phases it has. Show the calendar that tells when the various phases will appear.

Have pupils prepare a "Moon Watch" chart as shown:

Date and time of observation	Drawing of appearance of the moon	State of the sky

Ask pupils to record the date, draw the shape of the moon at the time of the observation and record the state of the sky as clear, cloudy, etc.

Note how the moon's appearance changes but the changes are always in a predictable way.

Move the discussion to a consideration of how our faces appear to others — sometimes bright and cheerful, sometimes dark and gloomy. Use the following questions as discussion starters:

    1. What kinds of faces do we like to see best?

    2. What effect does the expression we wear on our faces have on others who live with us?

Conclude the learning activity by having pupils draw a series of happy faces.

17. I WISH (Grades 3-6)
VALUE: ASPIRATIONS

A. Purpose: To encourage students to think realistically about their wishes and aspirations and to plan ways to achieve their fulfillment.

B. Materials: A copy of the book, "Wizard of Oz" by L. Frank Baum, a wishbone, a picture of a birthday cake with candles.

C. Procedure: Discuss with your class what it means to make a wish. Bring a wishbone to class and explain how two persons might make a wish. Then pull to see who gets the largest part of the wishbone and supposedly has his wish come true.

Also show your picture of the birthday cake and candles. Ask what the person whose birthday it is does before blowing out the candles. The obvious answer is "makes a wish."

Have pupils consider if just making a wish makes the wish come true. What does it take to make a wish come true?

Read those parts of "The Wizard of Oz" dealing with characters such as the Cowardly Lion. Have pupils listen especially for what the character's chief desire or wish was and what had to be done to make it come true.

Summarize by having pupils write down one or more of their wishes or aspirations and list systematically what they need to do to make them come true.

18. HONESTY HAIKU (Grades 3-6)
VALUE: HONESTY

A. Purpose: To encourage pupils to think about key words and ideas related to honesty.

B. Materials: Information about poetry forms of Haiku. A few model Haiku poems.

C. Procedure: Explain to your class that Haiku is a form of poetry of the Japanese people. It has three unrhymed lines. There are five syllables in the first and third lines and seven syllables in the second line. Although Japanese usually use this form when they write poetry related to nature, ask them to write poems about some aspect of being honest.

D. Variation: Use other themes such as kindness, patience, generosity, etc., about which pupils can write Haiku poetry.

19. EXAMINE THE CONSEQUENCES OR RESULTS (Grades 3-8)
VALUE: THOUGHTFUL ACTION

A. Purpose: To help pupils "think-through" what the consequences or results of their behavior will be.

B. Materials: A list of situations that are related to the daily experiences of your students. Newspaper headlines.

C. Procedure: Show the newspaper headlines to your class and discuss the news events related to them with your class. Then write the headings shown below on the chalkboard:

TODAY'S HEADLINES	PREDICTED RESULTS OR CONSEQUENCES

Write the general newspaper headlines as well as the headlines of a number of lesser newspaper articles in the left column.

Next encourage your class to predict what the consequences or results of the action reported in the story might be. Write these in the right column. If possible, follow the story in the newspaper during the next few days or weeks to see if the predictions made came true with a degree of accuracy.

Now make a second chart on the chalkboard similar to the first except substitute the words, "My Plans for Today" as the heading of the column. Have pupils each make a chart of this kind on a sheet of paper and fill in a few items in both the first and second columns. Ask them to make predictions about the consequences or results of their planned actions as thoughtfully and accurately as possible.

Conclude the activity by noting with your class that we can avoid unpleasant results or consequences by considering beforehand what they are likely to be and then by deciding not to perform the action that produces such unpleasant results.

20. VALUE CENTER (Grades 4-7)
VALUE: DEFINING VALUES

A. Purpose: To help students define their values by telling what various values mean to them.

B. Materials: A learning center area where pupils could write their responses during any free time they might have.

C. Procedure: Set up a "Value Center" in the corner of your classroom. Instruct pupils to use the center according to the regular schedule you have for such free-time activities.

Make a poster similar to that shown below to mount in the center area:

THINK ABOUT YOUR VALUES

Steps to follow:

1. Select a folder with a title in which you are interested.

2. Take a worksheet from the folder and complete the questions.

3. Place the completed worksheet in your personal folder.

On the table in the learning center, have two boxes of folders. In the left box have folders labeled with a wide variety of values. In the right box have folders labeled with the pupils' names.

Pupils should choose a worksheet from the folders in the value worksheet box and when they have completed it, place it in their own folder in the other box.

Value worksheets could be made up on topics such as the following:

| Friendship | Freedom | Honesty |
| Truth | Kindness | Promptness |

Use the following questions in developing the worksheet form:

Name _____   Date _____

Value:
    (Write this word in the blanks in the questions below before you begin answering them.)

1. What does the word _____ mean to you?
2. How important is _____ to you?
3. How do you presently show your _____?
4. List any ways in which you could show your _____ in a better way.

After each child has several worksheets completed in his folder, hold a private conference with him to discuss the results and encourage him in implementing his values.

21. DO CLOTHES MAKE THE PERSON?
(Grades 4-8)
VALUE: GENUINENESS

A. Purpose: To show pupils that what one is, is more important than what one wears.

B. Materials: Pictures of a wide range of persons in all kinds of costumes and uniforms from regular daily work clothes to elaborate formal dress. Bulletin board space, scissors. Construction paper.

C. Procedure: Ask your class the question, "Which is most important, the clothes a person wears, or what a person is really like?" Mount the following caption on the bulletin board:

WHAT ARE THESE PEOPLE LIKE?

Mount pictures of persons dressed in various costumes and have pupils describe what the people are like. Pupils will likely describe the persons in terms of what their costumes indicate they do, e.g., this person is a fireman, this person is a movie star, a baseball player, etc.

Next cut small oval holes in sheets of construction paper and place over the pictures of the persons in costume so that only the face of the person is visible as shown below.

Now ask pupils to tell what the persons are really like. This time, instead of looking at the clothes the person in the picture is wearing, the pupils will have to study only the faces of the persons pictured.

This time instead of telling what the people do judging from the clothes they wear, the pupils will need to look at the expressions on their faces to describe their personal characteristics.

Summarize the activity by discussing the greater importance of what a person is and not what a person wears.

22. HOW MUCH TV? (Grades 2-6)
VALUE: LIMITING TV VIEWING TIME

A. Purpose: To encourage pupils to consider the amount of time they spend watching TV and to weigh the alternatives.

B. Materials: Writing materials for a record form.

C. Procedure: Discuss the benefits of TV with your class. Point out the advantages of keeping informed about news and entertainment by sports events and other programs.

Note, too, with your class that sometimes people spend time watching TV when they could more properly be doing other things.

Have each pupil prepare a personal chart similar to that shown below:

MY TV VIEWING TIME CHART FOR ONE WEEK			
Date			Name
Beginning Time	Ending Time	Amount of Time	Possible Alternative Uses of Your Time

Have pupils keep a record of the amount of time they spend viewing TV for one week. Each time they record a time block of TV viewing, have them record at least one alternative use of their time.

Summarize the activity by encouraging pupils to consider the many interesting and valuable alternative ways one can use to avoid overuse of TV viewing.

23. PERSONAL PREFERENCES (Grades K-8)
VALUE: GOOD SELF-IMAGE

A. Purpose: To help pupils become more aware of the personal preferences they have.

B. Materials: Picture of each pupil, some type of construction paper and writing materials.

C. Procedure: Implement this learning activity shortly after school pictures have arrived. Have pupils use one of their pictures to paste on a sheet of poster or construction paper with the letters of the child's name printed vertically or diagonally in some manner similar to that shown below.

| M
 A
 R
 Y

 S
 M
 I
 T
 H | | M
 A
 R   Y
     O
    R
   S
    M
     I
      T
       H | |

Next have pupils think about things they like to do and other personal preferences they have as individuals to strengthen their sense of self-identity and self-image.

Have them choose things that begin with the letters of their name and complete the poster about themselves in a manner similar to that shown below:

M - mustard on hot dogs
A - apple pie
R - reading books
Y - yellow

S - swimming
M - music
I - ice cream
T - tomatoes
H - hamburgers

Have pupils show their completed posters to others in the class and allow the pupils opportunity to explain what they like about the things they have listed.

Display the completed posters in school or allow pupils to take them home to decorate their rooms.

Conclude the learning experience by discussing wide variety of preferences people have, the freedom we enjoy to exercise those preferences and the ways in which we can respect the personal preferences of one another.

24. ACCEPTING PRAISE GRACIOUSLY
(Grades 3-8)
  VALUE: GENUINENESS

A. Purpose: To help pupils accept praise without being proud or self-demeaning.

B. Materials: Various groups of students.

C. Procedure: Ask the pupils to list occasions when members of the school's student body receive awards or honors. Write these on the chalkboard as they are stated. You may wish to begin the list with a few very familiar occasions such as:

a pupil wins an athletic event, or

a pupil takes part in a musical contest and wins an award

When the pupils have extended the list of all-school awards, go on to list honors or awards that give recognition to smaller groups such as clubs or within classrooms. To stimulate the pupils' ideas in this area, you may begin by suggesting the following:

a pupil is elected to a club office

a pupil turns in an unusually fine report, etc.

After you have a sizeable list of situations in which students are given some praise or recognition, have the class form groups. Ask each group to select one of the situations listed and role play the awarding incident but have the pupil receiving the honor act in a self-demeaning way. Such as one who receives an honor for scholarship but to avoid accepting the praise for his/her efforts, acts as if what was done was worthless.

Next have the pupils repeat the role playing exercise but have the person receiving the award portray a pupil who is unduly proud because of the praise.

Follow the role playing exercise with a discussion of how difficult it is to accept praise graciously. Again make a list of suggestions on the chalkboard. Begin the list with ideas such as the following:

1. Say "Thank you" for the award or compliment.

2. Show that you appreciate ways others may have helped you.

Have the class add other suggestions.

After the discussion, have pupils role play the same situations again, this time portraying a gracious and appreciative way to accept praise without the extremes of pride on one hand or self-abasement on the other hand.

25. FINGERPRINTS (Grades 4-8)
VALUE: INDIVIDUALISM

A. Purpose: To strengthen the child's sense of personal identity as an individual distinct from others.

B. Materials: An ink stamp pad, 3 x 5 inch cards, learning center space.

C. Procedure: Use an ink stamp pad to have pupils in your class record their thumb prints on a class chart with their names of follows:

THE MEMBERS OF CLASS————————		
Mary	Peter	Dawn

Display the chart as an answer key in a learning center station.

Next have pupils each print a short paragraph on a 3 x 5 inch card about a topic of their own choice. Instead of signing the article with their name, have them stamp their thumb print at the bottom. Number the cards.

In the learning center, have the pupils look at the cards and try to identify the author by matching the thumb prints on them with those on the chart. Have them list their answers on a numbered answer sheet that corresponds to the numbers on the cards.

After all the pupils have had an opportunity to try to identify the authors, have each pupil claim his/her card and read it and the number to the class so they can check the correctness of their answers.

Summarize the activity by recalling how we not only have different fingerprints, but are different from one another in many other ways as well.

CHAPTER 2

Values that are more external and are often expressed in words and actions.

1. LOOK AT THE BRIGHT SIDE
(Grades K-4)
VALUE: CHEERFULNESS

A. Purpose: To help pupils see the difference between a positive, cheerful attitude and a negative, unpleasant attitude.

B. Materials: The following list of questions:

1. What's the weather like today?
2. How did you like the game?
3. Did you enjoy school today?

Other questions appropriate to your school situation.

C. Procedure: Initiate the discussion of cheerfulness with a smile. Discuss the fact that it is nicer to be with and work with others who have a cheerful outlook on life. Ask for a few volunteers to role play a situation in which one person provides a cheerful response and another an unhappy or unpleasant response to the same question.

Have two pupils step out into the hall and come in one at a time. Ask the first pupil to give a truthful and cheerful response to the question you select to ask. Ask the second pupil to give a truthful but unhappy or unpleasant response to the same question. Have the pupils exchange roles to avoid the possibility that they might be labeled one way or the other.

After your class has listened to both types of responses to several questions, have them evaluate the way the different responses affected them. Point out how one's cheerfulness affects others.

D. Variation: Have pupils actually play the role

of "Mr. Cheerful" or "Mr. Unpleasant" for a given period of time in the classroom and evaluate the results.

2. GOOD MANNERS MORNING (Grades 2-5)
VALUE: GOOD MANNERS

A. Purpose: To provide special opportunities for pupils to learn and practice good manners.

B. Materials: Chart making materials such as poster paper and felt pens of various colors.

C. Procedure: Set aside one morning per week as "Good Manners Morning." When introducing the idea, begin your GOOD MANNERS CHART by listing one rule for good manners on it in a manner similar to that shown below.

THE GOOD MANNERS CHART OF ROOM____
1. Don't interrupt--take turns talking. 2. Don't push in line--be patient. 3. Don't run in the hall--walk.

Encourage class members to make a special effort to practice the rule listed throughout the morning.

Add a new "rule" each week and continue to encourage pupils to practice these with care on the "Good Manners Morning" selected.

D. Variation: Hold an evaluation discussion at the end of the special morning and note with your class how the use of good manners makes the classroom a more pleasant place for all to live and work.

3. LET'S PUT FRUIT ON OUR HELPFULNESS TREE (Grades K-5)
VALUE: HELPFULNESS

A. Purpose: To encourage pupils to perform helpful deeds for others and recognize the helpful things others do for them.

B. Materials: Construction paper and bulletin board space.

C. Procedure: Make a "Helpfulness Tree" out of construction paper with only branches but not leaves or fruit.

Explain to the pupils that they can help the tree grow by adding leaves and fruit. Each time someone does something helpful for them, they should make a leaf or a type of fruit, write the person's name on it as well as what he/she did that was helpful and pin the leaf or fruit on the "Helpfulness Tree."

Encourage pupils to use construction paper of various colors and leaves of various shapes to add to the attractiveness of the display as well as to show that helpful deeds come in all ways.

After a number of leaves and types of fruit have been pinned up, discuss the following questions with your class:

1. How has the "Helpfulness Tree" helped you to be helpful to others?

2. Did you notice more of the helpful things others did for you while you were working on the helpfulness tree?

3. In what other ways could the class members show helpfulness to one another in addition to the ways already shown on the tree?

D. Variation: At the end of each day, or week, "pick" the fruit. Give the fruit picked to the pupil whose name appears on it as a reward for the help that was given as a token of appreciation from the person who was helped.

4. WHAT IS LEADERSHIP? (Grades 3-6)
VALUE: LEADERSHIP

A. Purpose: To help pupils develop a sense of the importance of wise leadership.

B. Materials: Pictures of many types of leaders, both good and bad.

C. Procedure: Begin by showing pictures of the following:
1. an orchestra leader
2. an airplane pilot
3. Adolph Hitler
4. the leaders of a street gang

Discuss how each of the leaders pictured directed the actions of others. For example: the orchestra leader coordinates the efforts of the members of the orchestra so they produce beautiful music in harmony; the airplane pilot directs all members of the plane's crew to work together for a safe journey; Adolph Hitler led his nation into war; the leader of a street gang leads his gang members into fights with others.

After showing the pictures explain how a good leader helps his followers to do good things and a bad leader challenges his followers to do bad things.

Next raise the question of the kinds of leaders we should choose to follow. How can we tell a good leader from a bad one? Have pupils suggest the qualities of a good leader and list these on the chalkboard.

D. Variation: Divide a chalkboard space into two sections using the headings shown below:

The Responsibilities of Leaders	The Responsibilities of Followers

Have the students suggest what should be written in the two columns. Conclude the exercise by pointing out the importance of wise leadership.

5. HELP WANTED (Grades 5-8)
VALUE: HELPFULNESS

A. Purpose: To help pupils realize how people engaged in various types of work help others through the work they do.

B. Materials: The "help-wanted" columns from the classified advertisements of the local newspaper. Chalkboard space.

C. Procedure: Write the following column headings on the chalkboard.

Job openings   How people engaged in this type of work serve others

Have pupils review the want ads and list the job openings in the left column.

Next discuss the type of work required of each

job opportunity and the skills needed to do the work. Follow this with a discussion of how the persons holding each of these types of jobs will be serving others. Point out how this service to others adds dignity to the work done and makes it especially satisfying. Relate the aspect of service to others as a point of key importance in the choice of one's career.

6. LIKE DOMINOES (Grades 1-8)
VALUE: ONE EVENT INFLUENCES THE NEXT

A. Purpose: To impress pupils with the idea that every event in our lives influences the events that follow.

B. Materials: A set of dominoes.

C. Procedure: Set the dominoes on end in a pattern similar to that shown below:

Have a pupil push over the first domino so that it falls against the second which pushes over the third, etc. Note with the class that what happens to one domino strongly influences the next.

Now set up the dominoes again with space at various points in the sequence as shown below:

Again have a pupil push over the first domino and note that all fall in sequence until a space intervenes. Then another push is needed to start the motion sequence again.

Use these examples to demonstrate how one action influences the next. If the action is good you can keep the action moving by spacing the actions close enough. If the action is not desirable, you can break the chain by spacing or delaying the next event.

Apply this concept to the lives of your pupils by having them consider times when momentum of a series of good events causes one to follow another. Also consider ways to break the momentum of a series of bad events by spacing or slowing them down.

7. SERVE AS A TRAVEL CONSULTANT
(Grades 4-8)
VALUE: CONSIDERING OPTIONS

A. Purpose: To encourage pupils to consider carefully how to plan a vacation.

B. Materials: A wide range of travel brochures, current prices of airlines, bus, train and automobile travel cost.

C. Procedure: Set up a "travel bureau consultant" corner in your classroom. Appoint various pupils to serve by turn as the travel consultant. Supply the corner "office" with a wide variety of travel brochures from a local travel agent.

Provide students with an imaginary sum of money such as $500 to spend for a vacation.

Ask them to consider their interests and the various possible ways to spend their vacation. Include options such as greater distance and more time spent "on the road" with less time at the destination vs. shorter distance and more time at the place to be visited; also include the options of more costly vs. less costly modes of travel.

After all students have had the opportunity to both serve as a tourist and a travel bureau consultant, evaluate the experience. Use the following questions to summarize:

1. Was it more difficult to seek or to give advise?

2. What factors were the most important to consider in reaching your decision?

D. Variation: Arrange a field trip to a local travel bureau office or invite a travel bureau consultant to speak to your class about his/her work.

8. ANALYZING INCONSISTENCIES (Grades 5-8)
VALUE: CONSISTENCY

A. Purpose: To help pupils realize where they are inconsistent and help them to be consistent.

B. Materials: A familiar story from the reading or literature text the pupils are using in class. Chalkboard.

C. Procedure: Place the following chart on the chalkboard:

	Consistent or Inconsistent	
Character's words or actions from the story	with the character's goals	with the character's other words and actions

Explain to the class that a person who is consistent will say and do things that are in harmony with his personal goals and with other things that he says and does. For example, a child who loves his parents will try to be obedient to them and will not say derogatory things about them. On the other hand, a person who is consistent may say that he loves his parents but still may do or say things that displease or dishonor them.

Next have the class choose a character from a story which they are assigned to read. Have pupils suggest five or more actions or statements of the character. Write these in the left column of the chart. Next ask if the statements or actions listed were in harmony with the kind of person the character was supposed to be or the kind of goals the character had. Mark a "c" for consistent and an "i" for inconsistent in the middle column.

Repeat the exercise for the third column by having the class analyze the harmony of the character's actions with other things he said and did.

Now have the class make a similar chart on a sheet of paper and record one thing that they do or say for each half hour during the school day. Near the close of the day, ask them to consider what they have written and mark the last two columns with a "c" or an "I".

Conclude the learning activity by discussing the value and importance of being consistent.

9. PLANNING YOUR TIME (Grades 5-8)
VALUE: EFFICIENT TIME USE

A. Purpose: To help pupils plan the efficient use of their time.

B. Materials: Time Use Planning Form. Chalkboard.

C. Procedure: Discuss with your class the importance of learning to use time efficiently. Develop a TIME USE PLANNING FORM such as the following for use by your class:

TIME USE PLANNING FORM OF _____
                                   name

                                   _____
                                   date

- -

TASK TO BE DONE:
MATERIALS NEEDED:
ESTIMATED TIME NEEDED TO COMPLETE:
ORDER OF PRIORITY:

- -

TASK TO BE DONE:
MATERIALS NEEDED:
ESTIMATED TIME NEEDED TO COMPLETE:
ORDER OF PRIORITY:

Write the form on the chalkboard and ask the students if there are any other items that should be added to it for their special needs. After the class has approved the form, make a duplicated master repeating the form as many times as possible on one sheet. Then run off a supply of copies for student use each day for one week.

At the end of the time, help the students see that planning time use helps them to complete their tasks more efficiently.

D. Variation: Contact a local industry that has a time use study expert. Invite this person to speak to your class about the way industry attempts to provide for efficient time use by its employees.

10. COURTESY MOBILES (Grades K-8)
VALUE: COURTESY

A. Purpose: To remind pupils to use common terms of politeness and courtesy regularly.

B. Materials: Mobile constructing materials including string, wire, sticks and cardboard.

C. Procedure: Write this short but well-known saying on the chalkboard:

POLITENESS IS TO DO AND SAY THE KINDEST THING IN THE KINDEST WAY.

Discuss the meaning of this saying with your class and ask them to list the common words they know that show politeness and the common things they do to show kindness. Write the lists on the chalkboard as the terms are mentioned. The lists will likely include the following:

POLITE WORDS	KIND DEEDS
Please	Open a door
Thank you	Pick up something
I'm sorry	Move up a chair

Show students how to make mobiles. Divide the class into groups and have each group make a "Courtesy Mobile" using either the Polite Words or Kind Deeds as the theme. Display the mobiles in your classroom as courtesy reminders.

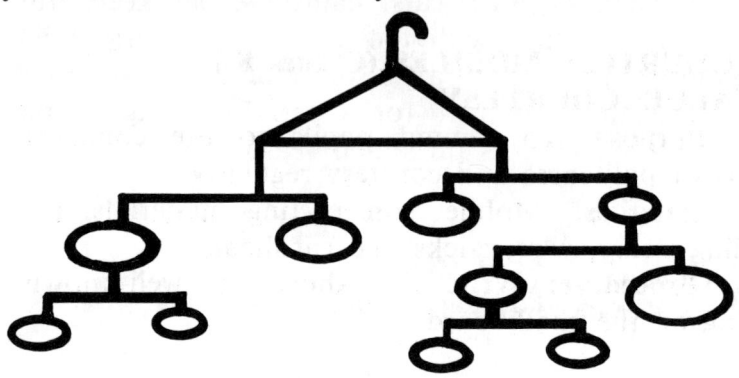

11. CHOOSING A PET (Grades K-5)
VALUE: RATIONAL CHOICES

A. Purpose: To help pupils make rational choices about pets.

B. Materials: Picture of various type of pets.

C. Procedure: Discuss the various types of animals that members of your class have as pets. Arrange these in chart form as shown below:

Kind of animal kept as a pet	Advantages of this kind of pet	Disadvantages of this kind of pet

Write the suggestions of the pupils on the chalkboard in the chart. You may also wish to use the bulletin board for this exercise so that you can mount pictures of pets rather than names. The suggestions of the pupils could then be put up in picture form, e.g. puppy spilling milk or in word form on strips of poster paper.

After you have listed several animals that are kept as pets such as dogs, cats, hamsters, parakeets, turtles, etc., together with their advantages and disadvantages, discuss how a person should choose which type of animal to have for a pet. Encourage pupils to base their choices on sound reasons.

12. A FOUR WAY TEST (Grades 3-8)
   VALUE: SPEECH CONTROL
   A. Purpose: To help pupils sense that what we say should meet a four way test.
   B. Materials: A scorecard for each pupil.
   C. Procedure: Use a duplicated sheet to make a scorecard similar to that shown below:

SCORECARD OF THE THINGS SAID					
By _____ name During the Week of _____ date					
Four Questions to Ask Yourself:	MON	TUES	WED	THURS	FRI
1. Is it the truth?					
2. Is it fair?					
3. Is it kind?					
4. Is it helpful?					
KEY: A - I said good things all day. B - I said good things almost all day. C - I said some things I shouldn't have today. D - I said many things I shouldn't have today.					

Provide a scorecard for each child and explain that everyone in the room (including the teacher) will spend a few minutes near the end of the school day thinking about all he/she said to others during that day. Then each person should mark each question using the key provided at the bottom of the scorecard. On Friday afternoon of the week in which the scorecard is used, conclude the activity by discussing ways in which we need to be careful of things we say. The following questions could be used to begin the discussion:

1. Should you repeat something about someone else just because it is true?
2. How can you tell if something you say about someone else is kind?
3. What should you do if you realize that something you have already said is not true?

13. A TIMELY TOPIC (Grades K-8)
VALUE: PUNCTUALITY

A. Purpose: To teach pupils how everyone depends on the punctuality of others.

B. Materials: A collection of pictures of buses, planes and trains. Several timetables of travel schedules followed by each of the public transportation systems serving your community. A sample appointment book and materials from which pupils can make an appointment book of their own.

C. Procedure: Arrange bulletin board display of bus, plane and train pictures and schedules under the caption: WHY MUST THEY BE ON TIME? Try to involve pupils in arranging the display.

Use the display as the basis for a class discussion

about ways in which your community depends on the services provided by public transportation systems. Develop a list of reasons why they must announce and keep schedules. What happens when buses, planes or trains are late?

Show the appointment book and explain why such appointment books are important for doctors, dentists and businessmen. Are the appointments important only to the doctors, etc., or do they also have an affect on many others?

Have each pupil make an appointment book of his/her own and record the chief events that require punctuality. Note with the class that although the appointment book tells us what we must do to be punctual, doing so is still up to us.

D. Variation: Check with local businessmen in an attempt to obtain small personal appointment books for your pupils.

14. WHO DO YOU TRUST? (Grades 4-8)
VALUE: TRUST

A. Purpose: To help pupils understand the meaning of trust and ways to exercise it.

B. Materials: Classroom clock or watch, writing materials.

C. Procedure: Begin this learning activity by asking someone what time it is. Ask if they trust the clock in the classroom or their watch. Establish the idea that the reason they do is because the clock or watch has faithfully given them the correct time in the past. Discuss under what circumstances a person would hesitate to trust his watch.

Ask the class to think of other ways in which we show trust. Use the following questions as guides:

How do people who ride on a bus trust the bus driver?

How do people who ride on an airplane show their trust in the plane and the pilot?

How do people who eat in a restaurant show their trust in the cook?

How does someone who hires a carpenter to fix his roof show his trust in the person he hires?

Next discuss the reasons why we trust our parents and our friends. Include the ideas that we trust people we know we can depend on, on people we know to be fair, truthful and honest.

Ask the pupils to make a list of persons they can trust and the reasons why they can do so on a chart similar to the one shown below:

Persons I can trust	Reasons why I trust them

Next list the names of some persons who trust you and tell why they do so.

Conclude the activity by discussing why it is important to have people we can trust and how we can build the trust of others in us.

15. LOST AND FOUND (Grades 3-6)
VALUE: HONESTY

A. Purpose: To help pupils realize that articles lost by someone should be returned if found.

B. Materials: Information about the "Lost and Found" system of your school.

C. Procedure: Begin by asking your pupils if they

have ever lost something they really treasured. If it was found by someone else and returned to them, how did they feel when they got the article back? Continue the discussion by using the following questions:

1. If you lose an article, does it still belong to you even if you have lost it?
2. If you find something that you know belongs to someone else, what should you do?
3. If you find something, and do not know to whom it belongs, what should you do?
4. Where does your school maintain its "Lost and Found" department?
5. If you find something and turn it in to the "Lost and Found" department and if no one claims it after a given period of time, what happens to the item?
6. How do you feel towards a person who returns an article to you that you have lost?
7. Why would keeping something you found without attempting to find its owner be dishonest?

D. Variation: Appoint a committee to assist in the operation of the school's "Lost and Found" department.

16. AGREEABLE OR DISAGREEABLE
(Grades 3-8)
VALUE: BEING AGREEABLE
A. Purpose: To help pupils realize that being disagreeable makes life unpleasant for both oneself and others.
B. Materials: Writing materials.
C. Procedure: Have the class write a story about

common experiences that might occur in one day of the life of a boy or girl about their age who is selfish, uncooperative and generally disagreeable. Ask the other half of the class to write about similar experiences of a child who is unselfish, cooperative, happy and generally agreeable.

When the pupils have finished their stories, group them in pairs, one from each half of the class to read their stories to one another.

Summarize the activity by discussing ways in which being disagreeable makes life unpleasant for both oneself and for others.

D. Variation: Role play the situations that the pupils have described in their papers.

17. A CONTEST (Grades K-4)
VALUE: KINDNESS

A. Purpose: To convince pupils that one can prove greater strength by being kind than by being forceful or mean.

B. Materials: A copy of the fable about the contest between the sun and the wind entitled, "Which is Stronger?" which may be found in most anthologies of children's literature.

C. Procedure: Begin the lesson by reading the fable to the class. Note with them what strategies the wind and the sun used to get the person to take off his coat. Use the following questions to promote thoughtful discussion:

1. How did the plan of the wind and the sun differ?
2. How did the man react when the wind blew harder and harder?

3. What kinds of things do we do when we want others to do what we say, that are like the blowing of the wind?

4. How did the man react when the sun began to shine gently and warmly?

5. What kinds of things do we sometimes do that are like the shining of the sun?

Conclude the learning activity by asking pupils to make a list of things they do on a chart like the one shown below:

Things we do that are like the wind	Things we do that are like the sun

After the charts are finished, summarize by having pupils tell which type of activities was most effective.

SECTION TWO

VALUES RELATED TO THE FAMILY

The family is the basic foundation undergirding the structure of society. The activities in this section will strengthen the values upon which this foundation rests.

1. MY FAMILY IS WHERE I BELONG
(Grades K-2)
VALUE: SENSE OF BELONGING

A. Purpose: To strengthen the child's sense of belonging by emphasizing his membership in a family group.

B. Materials: Bulletin board space, a wide range of pictures about family life and activities.

C. Procedure: Mount the caption, "WHAT FAMILY MEMBERS DO TOGETHER" on the bulletin board. Begin the picture display by putting up a few pictures of families doing things together such as eating together, praying together, enjoying leisure time activities together, etc. Have pupils add pictures of some activities their family has enjoyed together.

Provide opportunity for pupils to describe the family activity pictured. Encourage them to use plural possessive pronouns like we, our, etc., when speaking of their families.

Hold a class discussion about what it means to belong to a family and the kinds of things family members do with and for each other.

Have each child tell something nice about some member of his/her family.

Conclude the learning exercise by asking how they feel if they come home from school and no one is home; contrast this with how they feel when they have someone at home to welcome them.

2. WHAT PARENTS DO FOR US (Grades K-3)
VALUE: APPRECIATION FOR PARENTS

A. Purpose: To strengthen the appreciation children have for their parents by considering the many things that their parents do for them.

B. Materials: A beginning list of the things the parents of your pupils do for them. Art materials.

C. Procedure: On the chalkboard, write a beginning list of things that the parents of your pupils do for them. Include items such as the following:

> Provide a home for us to live in
> Provide beds and blankets
> Provide clothes for us to wear
> Provide the food we need
> Care for us when we are sick

Next have pupils think of other things their parents do for them and add these to the list. When the list is as long as you with your class can make it, ask, "Shall we make some 'Thank you' cards for them for everything they do for us?"

Allow each child to select a piece of construction paper of the color of his/her choice. Discuss the kinds of things pupils could write, draw or color on the cards that would convey appreciation to the parents for the things they do for their children.

When the project is finished, have the pupils take the "Thank You" cards home to their parents.

D. Variation: Hold a "Parents Appreciation" day. Invite the parents of your pupils to visit the classroom. Plan and present a short program including a few recitations, plays and songs that convey appreciation to the parents.

3. SEND A CARD (Grades 1-5)
VALUE: AFFECTION
A. Purpose: To encourage pupils to express their

affection for family members through sending cards to loved ones.

B. Materials: Construction paper, a list of special days and a supply of 3 x 5 inch cards.

C. Procedure: Give each child a 3 x 5 inch card. Have them make a list of days when it is particularly appropriate to send a card that expresses affection. Include the following:

> Mother's Day
> Father's Day
> Valentine's Day
> Christmas
> Easter, etc.

On the other side of the card have each child list the birthdates of parents, grandparents, brothers, sisters, aunts, uncles, their minister, the school principal, aged members of the community, etc.

Keep these cards in a handy place in your desk for ready reference.

Set aside a small work area, "A Thoughtful Corner" in your classroom where a child can go in any spare time, refer to his/her card in the file and make a card for someone special. Include construction paper, scissors, etc., for the pupils to use for this purpose. Keep a record of all cards made and sent.

4. HELPING AT HOME (Grades K-4)
VALUE: RESPONSIBILITY

A. Purpose: To help pupils develop a sense of responsibility for helping at home.

B. Materials: Five pages of regular paper used in

the classroom and a cover sheet of heavier construction paper.

C. Procedure: The project should be planned as a one week project with a little time each of five school days being used for it. Initiate the project by discussing with the class the kinds of things our parents and other adults do for us at home and have done for us in the past.

Next discuss the kinds of things we can now do for ourselves and the ways in which we can do things for others in our homes.

Distribute one sheet of paper to each student and have each student write the day of the week on the top line as follows:

Monday I helped at home by _____

_____

Then have the children write about or draw pictures of the ways they have helped at home in the morning before coming to school or ways in which they plan to help that afternoon or evening. Collect and save the papers when the exercise is completed.

Repeat this exercise for each of five consecutive school days. On the fifth day, hold a discussion using the following questions as starters:

1. How many of the tasks that we do at home must be done over and over again?
2. What task that we do are we doing only for ourselves? Why is this necessary?
3. Which tasks that we do are helpful to others? How does this make us feel? How does it make other family members feel?

Conclude the exercise by having the pupils make a cover with the title, "HELPING AT HOME" and a design of their own choosing.

Redistribute the pages you collected each day and staple each child's work together with the cover to form a booklet.

Have the pupils take the booklets home to show to and discuss with their parents.

5. WHERE HAVE YOU BEEN? (Grades 2-6)
VALUE: PROMPTNESS

A. Purpose: To help pupils realize how important it is to obey family rules about when to come home or to let their parents know where they are if they must be late.

B. Materials: A variety of pictures that show parents caring for children.

C. Procedure: Begin the lesson by showing the pictures of and discussing the many ways that parents show they care about their children.

Next point out that because parents care about their children, they often worry about them as well. Have the class suggest reasons why their parents might worry about them. It is likely some of the following situations would emerge:

1. If they are sick.
2. If they had an accident.
3. If they got lost, etc.

Focus on the worry that parents have when children do not come home when they are supposed to do so.

Have groups of pupils practice and present to the class the following role playing situations:

1. The child's school dismisses at 3:15 and the child comes home regularly at 3:40. Today she goes to her friend's house without telling her parents and forgets about the time until 5:00.

2. Two children tell their parents they will be playing on the school yard and will be home at 4:00. They change their minds and go to the park instead. There they play until dark.

Conclude the lesson by summarizing the feelings of parents when children do not come home on time. Emphasize the need for children to tell parents of their whereabouts and to be prompt in coming home on time.

D. Variation: Have a lesson on telephone use so children know how to call their parents to tell them if they have been delayed or when plans change.

6. ROOTS (Grades 6-8)
VALUE: APPRECIATION FOR ONE'S ANCESTRY

A. Purpose: To encourage pupils to become interested in and informed about their ancestors.

B. Materials: A copy of Alex Haley's book, ROOTS, or of the condensed version from the May and June, 1974, issues of the *Readers Digest*.

C. Procedure: Read to the students or have pupils read for themselves selected passages from ROOTS in either the complete book or condensed *Readers Digest* form.

Discuss the interest that people generally have in their ancestry and why it was particularly difficult for Alex Haley as an American Negro to learn about his ancestors.

Have the class members make a family tree of the people mentioned in the story.

Encourage students to make a family tree of their own ancestors.

7. PLEASANTNESS IN UNPLEASANTNESS
(Grades 3-8)
VALUE: HAPPINESS

A. Purpose: To help pupils realize that happiness can be found in unpleasant situations and unhappiness is often present in pleasant surroundings.

B. Materials: Bulletin board space.

C. Procedure: Introduce the idea that a family may live under very unpleasant circumstances from the standpoint of material possessions and yet be very happy. Also introduce the idea that a family that has everything it wants and more from the standpoint of material possessions may be very unhappy.

Mount the following caption on the bulletin board:

FINDING HAPPINESS

UNPLEASANT SITUATION	TYPE OF HAPPINESS THAT IS POSSIBLE

Have your class make a list of unpleasant situations such as the following:

A broken leg that compels you to stay in bed
Rain on a picnic day
Not enough money to buy the new baseball glove that you want, etc.

Add others as suggested by the class. Next ask the class to suggest ways in which happiness could possibly be found in even these unpleasant situations.

Summarize by encouraging pupils to look for happiness even in unpleasant situations in their own lives.

8. HOUSEKEEPING CORNER (Grades K-2)
VALUE: APPRECIATING PARENTS

A. Purpose: To strengthen the pupil's awareness of and build an appreciation for the many things that parents do for them.

B. Materials: A housekeeping corner in the classroom.

C. Procedure: Have pupils role play mothers and fathers taking care of and/or doing things with and for their children. This could include taking care of dolls the way parents take care of real babies.

Follow the activity with a discussion about the many things our parents and other adults do for us. As pupils suggest various items, record these on an experience chart as a class record.

You may wish to use the following items to begin your list:

1. Provide warm clothes for us to wear.
2. Provide the food we need and prepare our meals.
3. Provide a home for our family.
4. Care for us when we are sick.

Summarize the activity by encouraging pupils to thank their parents for the many things they do for them.

9. TASK CHOICES (Grades 4-8)
VALUE: COOPERATION

A. Purpose: To help pupils discern between tasks they like to do at home and those they prefer not to do.

B. Materials: Chart materials.

C. Procedure: Discuss the idea of cooperation and responsibility in the home and the ways members of a family or any other social group must work together and assume responsibility. Point out that one member of the group may like some tasks better while another may like some other tasks better. Make a chart of tasks to be done similar to the one shown below:

TASK TO BE DONE	PERSON RESPONSIBLE	LIKE OR DISLIKE	TIME REQUIRED

Encourage pupils to make the chart in school and complete it at home. Have pupils note that each person listed on the chart may have some tasks that are liked and some that are disliked.

Imagine a situation where a boy has the responsibility for making his bed, cutting the lawn and bringing out the garbage while his sister must do the dishes, fold the clothes and vacuum the carpets.

Suppose that the boy dislikes bringing out the garbage and the girl dislikes folding the clothes and that each task takes about an equal amount of time. Encourage them to arrange a change of jobs to test out if other jobs would be better liked and would be equally well done. Stress the idea of cooperation in having persons within the family responsible for the jobs they like best and are best able to do.

10. TABLE TALK TOPICS (Grades 3-8)
VALUE: OPEN COMMUNICATION

A. Purpose: To encourage open communication between children and their parents.

B. Materials: List of "Table Talk" topics.

C. Procedure: Make up a list of five "Table Talk" topics which pupils can discuss with their parents during mealtime.

Include topics that will lead to consideration of issues and values rather than simply future events or past occurrences.

Present the idea to the class by selecting a topic of current interest and asking if pupils are aware of how their parents feel about the issue. Encourage pupils to use the topic for mealtime discussion in their homes.

Have pupils turn in a report form similar to the following on 3 x 5 inch cards.

```
TABLE TALK TOPIC REPORT

Topic Discussed: _____

Lead to a worthwhile discussion
(circle one)

            Yes                    No


    _____         _____
         date                   name
```

Use the learning activity to stimulate discussion between your pupils and their parents but be careful to avoid intruding into the right of privacy of family conversations.

11. FAMILY MEMBERS BILL OF RIGHTS
(Grades 5-8)
VALUE: RESPECTING RIGHTS OF OTHER FAMILY MEMBERS

A. Purpose: To help pupils appreciate and respect the rights of other family members.

B. Materials: Bill of Rights of U.S. Constitution, writing materials.

C. Procedure: Refer to the Bill of the U.S. Constitution and note with your class the many rights that it guarantees for us.

Ask, "Do members of families have rights as well as the members of a country?" Follow this with a learning activity to write a FAMILY MEMBERS BILL OF RIGHTS. Use a form similar to that shown:

BILL OF RIGHTS OF MEMBERS OF THE _____ FAMILY	
FAMILY MEMBER	RIGHTS
Mother	To be respected and obeyed
	To have help in maintaining the home in good order
	To have members call or write a note when not able to be home for a meal

The comments included above are samples of the kinds of things pupils should be encouraged to include. Have pupils complete the Bill of Rights and take it home for discussion with the other members of their family.

D. Variation: Hold a panel discussion about the rights of various members of the family. Invite a teacher, a parent, or another adult to serve on the panel with a boy and a girl from your class to discuss the rights and obligations of various members of the family.

12. CARING FOR FAMILY PROPERTY
(Grades K-6)
VALUE: SHARING RESPONSIBILITY

A. Purpose: To strengthen the pupil's sense of family membership by calling to mind ways he/she contributes to a family's welfare by helping care for family property.

B. Materials: Drawing materials, chalkboard.

C. Procedure: Hold a class discussion about ways in which various members of a family help one another. Focus on the idea that all members of a family often use the things that belong to the whole family. All members of the family also help to care for such family property.

Ask your class to suggest various ways in which they have helped to care for the property of their family. List a large number of these on the chalkboard to suggest ideas to the class for use in drawing.

Next have the class draw a single picture or a series of pictures in comic strip fashion that illustrates how they have helped care for some article of family property and thus contributed to family well-being.

When the pictures are completed, display them on

the bulletin board under the caption, "WE ALL HELP AT HOME."

13. COMIC STRIPS SPEAK (Grades 3-8)
VALUE: GOOD COMMUNICATION

A. Purpose: To dramatize the idea of the importance of good communication in the family.

B. Materials: A variety of comic strips from the newspaper, blank white paper, glue.

C. Procedure: Have pupils select a comic strip of their favorite characters and ask pupils to copy down the words spoken by each of the characters.

Next have the pupils cut out shapes of white paper to match the shape of the conversation "balloons" and glue them in place to provide blank conversation areas.

When all pupils have completed blanking out the conversations, hold a discussion on the meaninglessness of the comic strips.

Next have pupils exchange the comic strips to avoid any trace of pupils remembering what had previously been said by the characters.

Ask pupils to use some scratch paper to make up several different sequences of conversation that would fit the comic strip characters they now have.

Have them select the best sequence and write it in conversation bubbles.

After these have been completed, have pupils return the comic strips to their original owners. Again hold a class discussion on the meaning that was added or changed by means of the new set of words used. Move the discussion to the importance of good communication. Ask questions such as the following:

1. How are the comic strips with blank word balloons like a home when members of the family don't speak together?

2. Have you ever had a friend with whom you had a quarrel which ended by not speaking to one another? How did you feel? How did you and your friend decide to end the wall of silence?

14. SHOWING LOVE (Grades K-4)
VALUE: LOVE

A. Purpose: To help pupils realize that there are many ways to show our love to others.

B. Materials: Bulletin board space, magazines, scissors.

C. Procedure: Ask your class what it means to have a favorite toy or book. Try to bring out the idea that an article that is one's "favorite" is valued, that is, it is important and is given special care.

Next ask what it means to love another person such as parents, other family members and special friends. This time bring out the idea that we truly value the persons we love. Such persons are important to us. We spend time with them and do things for them. We share the things we have with them.

Mount the following bulletin board caption together with a large heart as follows:

Invite pupils to find and cut out pictures, or draw pictures that show love in action. Mount these on the bulletin board in a large collage around the central caption and heart.

Summarize the activity by emphasizing the many thoughtful ways we can use to show we love others.

SECTION THREE

VALUES RELATED TO OUR HUMAN RELATIONSHIPS

All the relationships we have with other human beings are influenced by the values we hold. The activities in this section provide opportunity for pupils to understand and practice values crucial to successful human relationships.

1. THE BLIND MEN AND THE ELEPHANT
(Grades 4-8)
VALUE: RESPECTING DIFFERENT POINTS OF VIEW

A. Purpose: To enable the pupils to understand that the same issue may look different to different people.

B. Materials: A copy of the familiar poem, "The Blind Men and the Elephant" and a short news item about a local issue of which people hold different opinions.

C. Procedure: Read the poem, "The Blind Men and the Elephant" to your class and discuss its meaning with them. Use the following questions as discussion starters:

    1. What different conclusions did each of the blind men draw about what an elephant is like?

    2. Why did their conclusions differ?

    3. Could you tell what an elephant is really like by putting all their points of view together?

Next read the news item about the local issue and discuss different points of view that people have about it. Discuss what might have caused these different points of view. Make a list of the reasons why we should be understanding and respect the views of others even though they may be different than our own.

D. Variation: Hold a class debate about the issue and try to identify the reasons why each point of view may be upheld. Conclude the debate with a discussion of why people have differences of opinion and why we should respect the opinions of one another.

2. WINNERS OR LOSERS (Grades 5-8)
VALUE: SPORTSMANSHIP

A. Purpose: To help pupils realize that good sportsmanship is more important than winning or losing.

B. Materials: Letter writing materials.

C. Procedure: Discuss the idea of good sportsmanship. What is it? How can you tell if the players in a game or the spectators watching it are showing good sportsmanship?

Make a list of the kinds of things that are the most common evidences of poor sportsmanship at your school. Appoint a number of pupils to dramatize or role play each of these negative examples and have the class evaluate them by suggesting ways in which the poor sportsmanship demonstrated could be improved.

D. Variation: After a school game, have the members of your class write letters of commendation to players, cheerleaders or officials that exhibited particularly good sportsmanship. If the sportsmanship of a game was poor on the part of someone participating, ask your pupils to write that person a letter also asking that his/her sportsmanship be improved at the next sports event.

3. APPRECIATION TIME (Grades 3-8)
VALUE: APPRECIATION OF OTHERS

A. Purpose: To encourage pupils to express their appreciation of others to them by providing guided practice in doing so.

B. Materials: A small alarm clock. A supply of "Appreciation Cards."

C. Procedure: Recognize with your class how often others do nice things for us, yet how rarely we express our appreciation to them. Note also that we sometimes feel awkward or self-conscious when we receive a compliment or express appreciation to someone else. If we do so more frequently, however, we will feel more comfortable doing so.

Tell the pupils that you have set the alarm clock to go off at some time during the day. When that happens, you will pass out an "appreciation card" to each student. At that time have each pupil write down a compliment and/or a few words of appreciation to the person on his/her right (or some other classroom pattern so that everyone fills out and receives a card). Use a form such as the following:

APPRECIATION CARD
To:
Signature

To help students begin, write a few opening sentence stems on the chalkboard such as:

    Thank you for ......
    One thing I really like about you is......
    I really appreciate that you......

D. Variation: Hold a class discussion about the way giving and/or receiving a note of appreciation makes us feel. Make a resolution to show appreciation to others whenever you can honestly do so.

4. LET'S PLAY ANN LANDERS (Grades 3-7)
VALUE: EMPATHY

A. Purpose: To allow pupils opportunity to express their understanding of the problems of others.

B. Materials: Bulletin board space. Pen or pencils and writing paper.

C. Procedure: Introduce the lesson by reminding the class that everyone has problems and concerns at some time in their lives. We can often help others the most at such times of trouble if we try to understand how they feel.

Read the following imaginary letter to Ann Landers to the class:

Dear Ann Landers:

I'm just an average student in school but I don't like to do homework so my grades aren't very good. Yesterday I failed a test and now my folks won't let me watch TV for a week. What can I do?

(Signed) a sad student

Next tell the class you will put the letter up on the bulletin board. Put it under the heading, "ANN LANDERS SAYS". Tell the students to imagine they are Ann Landers and to write letters to "Dear Sad" giving their advice. Have them mount their letters on the bulletin board so that others can read them when they have free time. Stress the idea of "feeling with" the sad student.

D. Variation: Have pupils write anonymous letters to Ann Landers requesting advice on some problem they are experiencing. Have a special mailbox on your desk in which they can be mailed. Have the class respond with their suggestions in the form of letters of advice. Emphasize the need for understanding and sympathetic answers.

5. EMPLOYER--EMPLOYEE RELATIONSHIPS (Grades 5-8)
VALUE: RESPECT

A. Purpose: To help pupils understand that employers and employees show respect for one another by seeking the good of one another.

B. Materials: Several employer--employee situations written on 3 x 5 inch cards for committee use.

C. Procedure: Raise the issue of how employers can and should seek the welfare of their employees. Use the following situations (from your set of 3 x 5 inch cards) as the basis for this learning activity.

Situation One: You work in a small grocery store owned by the manager who operates it with the help of his wife. You are the only paid employee and have worked for them for many years.

Situation Two: You work the night shift on an assembly line in a factory that makes machine parts. You know the other men on your "line" and your foreman. The company is operated by a large corporation of several hundred stockholders through a board of directors whose names are listed on a bronze plaque at the entrance to the main building.

Situation Three: You baby-sit regularly once a week for a neighboring family.

Situations Four through Ten: Complete your set of 3 x 5 inch cards each listing an employer--employee situation familiar to the students in your class.

Divide your class into small discussion groups and give each group a card. Ask the pupils to discuss the question, "How can the employer in each case show respect and consideration for the needs and feelings of the employee as a person?" After a specific length of time, ask a representative of each small group to present the conclusions of their group to the class.

D. Variation: Assign each situation to a committee of students to role play in ways that show respect on the part of the employer for the employee as well as in ways that do not. Discuss the results with the total class.

6. I'M A MEMBER (Grades 4-8)
VALUE: MEMBERSHIP

A. Purpose: To help pupils appreciate the advantages of being a member of various groups.

B. Materials: Pictures of various groups such as a city council in session, a church congregation, a basketball team practicing, etc. Bulletin board space.

C. Procedure: Mount the caption, "I'M A MEMBER" on the bulletin board. Begin the discussion by holding up the first picture you have of a "group" such as a city council. Ask how one becomes a member of the group (through election) and what the members of the group do together (make laws). After discussing the picture, mount it on the bulletin board. Discuss and mount the other pictures

2. What do you think of his methods of doing so? Why?

3. Do you think Robin Hood's way of trying to solve the problem would work today? Why or why not?

Next discuss the difference between the way of life of the rich and the poor today. Consider how people live today and how the church and government have been trying to solve the problem of poverty.

D. Variation: Appoint a committee to interview some poor families in your community to learn about the problems they face. Have another committee interview government agencies, social workers or church leaders who work to solve the problems caused by poverty to learn of their methods and efforts.

13. HELPERS CLUB (Grades K-8)
    VALUE: HELPFULNESS

A. Purpose: To provide opportunity for pupils to volunteer their time and abilities to help others.

B. Materials: 3 x 5 inch cards to be used as membership enrollment forms. A list of students in the schools or adults in the school community who need help, would appreciate a cheerful letter, a visit, etc.

C. Procedure: Announce to your class that you are starting a new club in your classroom and that anyone interested may enroll as a member. The title of the club will be the HELPERS CLUB (or a similar name chosen by the group). Use the 3 x 5 inch cards as membership enrollment forms.

With the help of club members, formulate a list

Next hold an imaginary potlatch by "giving away" the slips of paper as representatives of the actual objects.

Summarize the activity by holding a discussion about generosity. Use the following questions as discussion starters:

1. Did you really decide to "give away" your most valuable possession?
2. How did it make you feel when you "gave" it away?
3. If you gave it away so others would note the importance of your gift, were you really being generous?
4. What is the difference between being selfish and being generous?

Conclude by pointing out the importance of being genuine in our generosity.

12. CONSIDER ROBIN HOOD (Grades 5-8)
VALUE: CARING FOR THE POOR

A. Purpose: To help students develop awareness of the problems of the poor and the best ways to help them.

B. Materials: A few tales about the life of Robin Hood from your library or literature books.

C. Procedure: Read a story about Robin Hood to your class or have them read such a story for themselves. Discuss the way Robin Hood tried to help the poor people of his day by stealing from people who were rich. Use the following questions as discussion starters:

1. What do you think of Robin Hood's goal to help the poor? Why?

After using the poem and the projector to focus the attention of the class on the idea of shadows, move the discussion to the idea of how young children will sometimes follow their parents or older brothers and sisters around. They will often try to do just what the older person is doing.

When younger children watch what we are doing and try to do the same, emphasize the idea that we must be especially careful to provide good models for them to follow.

D. Variation: Plan to use this learning activity during the early morning or late afternoon of the school day so that pupils can observe the shadows of trees, the flagpole, etc., as well as of themselves on the school playground as an introduction to the lesson.

11. POTLATCH (Grades 4-8)
VALUE: GENEROSITY

A. Purpose: To develop the child's sense of genuine generosity.

B. Materials: Information about the Indian custom of holding potlatches where one would show his greatness by giving away the biggest and most valuable things he owns.

C. Procedure: Make a study with your class of the Indian custom of holding potlatches.

Note how the prestige of the individual was enhanced by the size and value of the gifts given.

Have the pupils imagine that your class is going to hold a potlatch. Ask them to make a list of the five most valuable possessions they have on separate slips of paper and choose persons to whom they would give them.

"because" statements. Help the pupils to summarize the kinds of things that make one happy and provide satisfaction. Relate these to actions that are right, good and of service to self and others.

Next have pupils turn all their cards over and reread the things that made them unhappy or dissatisfied together with the "because" for each.

Again help them to summarize the reasons why things make them unhappy or do not provide satisfaction.

Conclude the activity by encouraging the pupils to "think through" the reasons for their actions in order that they may choose and do things thoughtfully and be more aware of the "because" or reason why actions provide happy or unhappy results.

10. SHADOWS (Grades K-4)
VALUE: BEING GOOD MODELS

A. Purpose: To impress pupils with the responsibility of being good models for others.

B. Materials: A copy of the poem, "My Shadow" by Robert Louis Stevenson which may be found in most anthologies of children's poems or in Childcraft Volume I. A filmstrip projector.

C. Procedure: Read the poem, "My Shadow" to the class and discuss the way a shadow goes with you and does whatever you do.

Next use the filmstrip projector to shine a beam of light against a blank wall. Have several children stand in the beam of light by turn (without looking into the light beam) so the shadow of their profile shows on the wall. Have the other pupils note how they can tell from the shadow who the person casting the shadow is.

C. Procedure: On the chalkboard draw a design of a 3 x 5 inch card as follows:

(Front Side)

| date | name |

Today I did something with which I was happy and satisfied.

It was_____

_____

_____

I was happy and satisfied with this because_____
_____

(Back Side)

The thing I did today that I was most unhappy and dissatisfied with was _____
_____
_____
_____

I was unhappy and dissatisfied with this because _____
_____

Near the end of the school day have each pupil fill out both sides of a 3 x 5 inch card. Collect them when the pupils have finished.

Repeat this each day for a school week. Then select a time when you can re-distribute the cards and ask each pupil to place all five cards with the front side up and reread the things with which he/she felt happiest and most satisfied. Then discuss the parents again, put the following column heading on the chalkboard:

Things children one or two years old can do	Things that others need to do for them

After the class has suggested a number of items and you have written these in the proper column on the chalkboard, use the following questions to culminate the lesson:

1. Did you enjoy doing something for a little child? Why or why not?
2. Do you think that those persons who cared for you when you were little enjoyed everything they had to do for you? If not, why did they do them?
3. Why do parents and others who care for little children need both love and a sense of responsibility?

D. Variation: Take your class on a field trip to a nursery school and observe the way the teachers there care for and teach the children. Ask the instructor to talk to your class about things they should and should not do in caring for small children.

9. BECAUSE (Grades 5-8)
VALUE: THOUGHTFUL ACTION

A. Purpose: To encourage pupils to "think through" the basis for their action.

B. Materials: Chalkboard and a supply of 3 x 5 inch cards.

Use the quarrels of cattlemen and sheepherders as an example of how different persons or groups have conflicting interests. Have pupils do research about this period of history in the school library and use the information they find as the basis for a play. Have pupils analyze the roles they played to see if there would have been any way to help the opposing parties understand one another's point of view. Conclude the learning activity by discussing the importance of understanding the point of view of others at times of conflict or disagreement.

D. Variation: Select a conflict situation that arises on the school playground, in the community or in the news generally and dramatize the situation after studying the issues. Again analyze the differences that become evident between the two sides. Conclude the learning activity by having the class note how difficult yet important it is to see both sides of a problem situation so that differences can be resolved.

8. LITTLE PEOPLE (Grades 3-6)
VALUE: CARING FOR SMALL CHILDREN

A. Purpose: To encourage pupils to care for smaller children and keep them from danger.

B. Materials: Two or more little children visit (perhaps the little brothers or sisters of class members), who have just learned to walk.

C. Procedure: Arrange to have the little children visit your classroom for an hour or two. During this time the class members may be both generally going about their regular studies and noticing how the little children would pick up things not seeming to realize if they are harmful or not, how they need care in entertaining themselves, etc.

After the children have been picked up by their

you have pointing out what it means to be a member of each group represented. Tell the class the groups of which you are a member and what this membership means to you.

Next ask each member of the class to make a list of the groups of which each is a member on a chart such as the following:

Groups of which I am a member	Obligations of Membership	Advantages of Membership

Have the class imagine what it would be like NOT to be a member of any group. Discuss how the groups we are members of help make our lives richer and more meaningful.

D. Variation: Ask a member of some club or community organization to come speak to your class about the organization he/she represents and the reasons that person values his/her membership in the group.

7. CATTLEMEN vs. SHEEPHERDERS (Grades 5-8)
VALUE: UNDERSTANDING

A. Purpose: To help pupils realize that there are two sides to every argument and it is difficult but important to see the other person's point of view.

B. Materials: Research materials about the conflicts between cattlemen and sheepherders at the time of the settlement of the west.

C. Procedure: Introduce the idea of how difficult it is to understand another person's point of view.

of activities that your group could do to help others.

Next make a study of the persons in your school or community that are in need of help and have volunteers from your club membership offer and supply the help.

D. Variation: Work with your local chapter of the American Red Cross, a local church or other service agency to learn of some service project your class could carry out that would be of benefit to the community generally or some group in it.

14. WAR OR PEACE (Grades 4-7)
VALUE: APPRECIATING PEACE

A. Purpose: To encourage students to compare war and peace by listing descriptive words related to each.

B. Materials: A thesaurus or dictionary of synonyms and antonyms and the chalkboard.

C. Procedure: Write the following column headings on the chalkboard:

WHEN I THINK OF	
PEACE, I think of . . .	WAR, I think of . . .

Ask the class what descriptive words come to mind when they think of peace. As pupils respond with a few terms, list them on the chalkboard in the left column. After you have five or six written in that column, ask the class what they think of when they think of war. Again list several of the students' suggestions on the chalkboard as they are mentioned.

Divide the class into two teams and ask them to think up or look up words appropriate to their column. Have each team select a student to write on the chalkboard the terms they feel are appropriate.

Set a time limit of about 15 minutes to see which group can list the greatest number of terms. Then tabulate the number written up by each team and draw a line across the bottom of the space used.

Next have the pupils exchange columns and attempt to think of words to add to the lists without being redundant. After a second time period, tabulate again to find the winning team.

Summarize the activity by looking at the terms of each list and note the contrast with the desirable terms being in the peace column and the undesirable terms being in the war column.

D. Variation: Use other terms that could be readily contrasted for column headings such as love and hate, liberty and oppression, etc.

15. WHAT'S IN A NAME? (Grades 3-8)
VALUE: FRIENDSHIP

A. Purpose: To encourage students to remember and use the names of their friends.

B. Materials: Writing materials.

C. Procedure: Begin the lesson by reviewing with your class, the proper way to introduce a friend of yours to someone else. Have pupils practice making introductions to one another.

Next note that the use of a person's name is very important in making and keeping friends. Remind your class of the following guidelines for the use of your friend's name:

1. Call the person by name as often as possible.
2. Know the person's first, middle and last name.
3. Sometimes people have nicknames but never call a person by his nickname unless he likes it.

Make a chart of your friend's names including the following information:

First name-
Middle name-
Last name-
Nickname-
Something I like about my friend-

Summarize the activity by reviewing the best ways to make and keep friends.

D. Variation: Have your students check the local telephone book to try to determine the five or ten names that are most common in your community.

**16. CHOICES BETWEEN OPPOSITES (Grades 4-8)
VALUE: CONSIDERING ALTERNATIVES**

A. Purpose: To help pupils realize that there may be many different alternative solutions to a quarrel.

B. Materials: Chalkboard. A quarrel between two students or an issue on which opinion seems to have polarized.

C. Procedure: Draw a line on the chalkboard about six feet long and write "Yes" on one end and "No" on the other. Draw another line and write "white" on one end and "black" on the other.

From your class solicit the idea that between the yes and the no, one could write the word "maybe" and between the black and white one could put all different shades of gray.

Next consider a current issue or question, and place one view at one end of the line and the opposite view on the other end. Now have pupils list as many options as possible that lie between these two opposing points of view. Note with your class that there are many possible views that lie between the two opposing points of view first listed.

Next identify the quarrel between the students. Write one point of view at one end of a line on the chalkboard and the other point of view on the other end. Now have the class suggest as many solutions as possible that lie between these two extreme points of view. Try to get the persons holding the extreme and opposing points of view in the quarrel to modify their positions and agree on an intermediate solution.

17. DON'T EMBARRASS OTHERS (Grades 5-8)
VALUE: AVOIDING EMBARRASSMENT

A. Purpose: To make pupils aware of the kinds of things that they do that might cause embarrassment to others and to avoid them.

B. Materials: List of situations that could be embarrassing to your students.

C. Procedure: Begin by acknowledging that no one likes to be embarrassed in front of others. Use the list of situations you have formulated to note with your class ways in which we can be embarrassed by others such as:

1. When someone says something degrading

about our appearance, e.g., Did you ever notice how large _____'s ears are?

2. When someone says something about a personal habit that we are trying to keep secret, e.g., Did you know that _____ sleeps with his toy bear or wets the bed?

3. When someone says something about something or someone we secretly like, e.g., Did you know that _____ would like to be _____'s boyfriend?

Since nearly everyone hates to be embarrassed by or in front of others, point out that we must all be careful to avoid embarrassing anyone by the things we say or do.

Divide your class into groups of three to five students each. Ask them to share with one another a time when they were embarrassed. Have them plan to role play two situations:

1. Role play the embarrassing situation.
2. Role play a kinder way to handle the situation.

Summarize the learning activity by emphasizing that to embarrass someone is a thoughtless and unkind thing to do.

18. SAY SOMETHING NICE (Grades 4-8)
   VALUE: COMPLIMENTING OTHERS
   A. Purpose: To help pupils expand the list of terms they use to compliment others.
   B. Materials: Chalkboard, writing materials, Thesaurus, dictionaries.
   C. Procedure: Remind your class that we all like to have someone tell us that we are nice, that we look well or have done something worthwhile. Write

the caption, "ONE HUNDRED WAYS TO SAY SOMETHING NICE", on the chalkboard.

Next start the list by writing the following words or chart phrases on the board:
  Terrific
  You made that look easy
  Not bad
  Good for you

Now challenge the class to see if they can expand the list to a total of one hundred ways to say something nice. Have them use a thesaurus, dictionary or other sources to locate words needed.

Conclude the exercise by encouraging students to put the terms they have listed to regular use.

19. COMPLIMENT TIME (Grades K-3)
VALUE: GIVING COMPLIMENTS

A. Purpose: To provide regular opportunity for pupils to give compliments to one another.

B. Materials: An alarm clock.

C. Procedure: Set the alarm clock to go off at a specific and appropriate time during the school day when pupils can lay aside their regular work for a few minutes and take time to give a compliment to someone else.

When you introduce the activity for the first time, you may wish to set up the sequence in such a way that every person gives a compliment to the person seated on his right, left, before or behind him in such a way that fits the seating arrangement in your classroom. The compliments may be given quietly so only the person receiving the compliment hears it, you may have pupils express these in such a way that all can hear.

In preparation for this exercise, have pupils notice nice things about one another that can be used as the basis for the compliments to be given.

20. PERSONS OR OBJECTS (Grades 3-8)
VALUE: IMPORTANCE OF PERSONS

A. Purpose: To help pupils realize that persons are of far greater value than objects.

B. Materials: Number of circumstances when a person must choose between valuing an object or a person most highly.

C. Procedure: Write the caption, "PERSONS OR OBJECTS, WHICH DO YOU CHOOSE?" on the chalkboard. Under this caption mount two sub-titles as follows:

OBJECTS	PERSONS
My favorite baseball glove	My friend
My bicycle	My brother
My best sweater	My sister

Add other choices as they are suggested by the class. When a sizeable list has been formulated, discuss the matter of choosing between an object or a person. Note with your class that difficult as it may sometimes be, it is important to place a greater value on persons than on objects.

D. Variation: Divide the class into groups of four or five pupils each and have each group dramatize a situation in which a choice must be made between caring more for an object or a person. Follow the dramatization with a discussion to evaluate the results.

21. NO MAN IS AN ISLAND (Grades 5-8)
VALUE: INTERDEPENDENCE

A. Purpose: To increase the pupils awareness of the interdependence of all human beings.

B. Materials: A group of pictures of islands including small desert islands, islands of the South Pacific, etc.

C. Procedure: Show your class the pictures you have of islands and note the characteristics of an island as follows:
  1. Separate from the mainland.
  2. Separate from other islands.
  3. Doesn't depend on anyone for anything.
  4. Continues to exist only by and for itself.

Next refer to the quote of John Donne who wrote many books of Devotions and poetry during the 1500's which points out that "no man is an island." Consider with your class the many ways in which persons differ from islands and ways in which our interdependence with other persons makes life more pleasant.

Try to identify things that make our relationships with others unpleasant and suggest ways in which such problems could be resolved.

Conclude the learning activity by having students write a theme using one of the two following titles:
  I WISH I WERE AN ISLAND, OR
  I'M GLAD I'M NOT AN ISLAND.
Have the students share the themes they write.

22. THINGS DONE BY AND FOR OTHERS (Grades 3-8)
VALUE: HELPING AND BEING HELPED

A. Purpose: To encourage pupils to willingly help

others and graciously accept things done for them.

B. Materials: Chalkboard, writing materials.

C. Procedure: Write the following column headings on the chalkboard:

Things we can do for ourselves	Things others do for us	Things we can do for others

Discuss the following questions with your class (answers will depend on maturity level of your pupils):

1. What kinds of things can we do for ourselves?
2. Why should we try to do as many things for ourselves as possible?
3. When should we allow others to do things for us rather than attempt them ourselves?

Have pupils copy the heading of the three columns on a sheet of paper. Then have them write two items from their own experience in each column during the coming week.

Summarize the activity by pointing out the need we have to distinguish between the things we can do for ourselves, what we need others to do for us, and what we can do for others.

D. Variation: After identifying some of the needs of others in your school community, plan together and set up a system whereby the class can work together to do something for them.

23. SHARED INTEREST GROUPS (Grades 2-8)
VALUE: FRIENDSHIP—COOPERATION

A. Purpose: To encourage pupils to improve their skills of cooperation by providing opportunity for those who have common interests to work together.

B. Materials: Interest inventory.

C. Procedure: Prepare an interest inventory such as the following:

INTEREST INVENTORY OF _____
                                NAME

My favorite sport is_____.
My favorite subject in school is_____.
My favorite food is_____.
My favorite TV program is_____.
My favorite animal is_____.

(Add other topics appropriate to your class and age level)

Tabulate the results after the students have completed the inventory. Group the pupils in the class according to the interests they share. Have the groups meet for an average of four or five times to discuss their common interests.

Then regroup on the basis of another category of the interest inventory.

Summarize the activity by noting that persons with common interests often have much to talk about and often establish friendships on the basis of their mutual interests.

D. Variation: Use the "Shared Interest Groups" system as the basis for cafeteria or noon lunch program seating arrangements to encourage friendships and develop communication skills.

24. MAKING INTRODUCTIONS (Grades 3-6)
VALUE: COURTESY

A. Purpose: To teach pupils the proper way to make introductions and to provide practice in doing so.

B. Materials: A school "Open-House" or other time when pupils and parents are at school together.

C. Procedure: Before a time when parents will be visiting your school at an "Open House" or other similar time, hold a practice session to teach pupils how to introduce their parents to you as teacher, to their friends or their friends' parents.

Role play the introductions so that pupils have an opportunity to gain confidence in doing so.

At the school "Open-House" set up the situation in such a way that pupils will have the opportunity and responsibility to make the introductions.

D. Variation: If no "Open-House" is planned where making such introductions is possible, consider other opportunities to have pupils introduce their parent(s) to you such as at the following:

An athletic event when the child and his/her parents are present as well as yourself.

Some other type of church or community event where you have the opportunity to meet the child's parents.

25. TELEPHONE MANNERS (Grades K-4)
VALUE: COURTESY

A. Purpose: To instruct students in common telephone courtesies and provide exercise in their use.

B. Materials: A set of telephones, play or real, for classroom use. Poster paper, learning center area.

C. Procedure: Review the rules for proper telephone use including the common courtesies that should be exercised. Make two copies of these rules on posters such as the following:

RULES FOR COURTEOUS TELEPHONE USE

1. Make social calls at a time when it would be convenient for the person called. (e.g. Avoid meal times.)
2. Honor reasonable time limits.
3. Make business calls in a friendly but business-like way.
4. Listen for a dial tone. If you are on a party line and someone else is talking, hang up the receiver quietly.

Solicit added rules from your class and complete the posters. Place the telephones in a learning center area and place a poster of rules by each.

Have pupils practice using the telephones to implement the rules for courtesy telephone use.

D. Variation: Contact the local telephone company for brochures about proper telephone use. Some companies also supply a set of telephones and a switchboard for classroom use.

Teach pupils important numbers and the proper process to follow when making emergency calls.

SECTION FOUR

VALUES RELATED TO PERSONAL HEALTH

Each day we make choices and decisions that affect our physical and mental well-being. The activites included in this section will help students develop sound values in the area of personal health.

1. SHOULD I SMOKE? (Grades 4-8)
VALUE: NON-SMOKING

A. Purpose: To help pupils understand the potential danger to health if one smokes and to choose for non-smoking.

B. Materials: Statistics about the relationship of smoking and lung cancer, heart disease, and other health problems. Bulletin board space, 3 x 5 inch cards.

C. Procedure: Mount the caption shown below on your bulletin board:

TO SMOKE OR NOT TO SMOKE....
THESE ARE THE QUESTIONS:
<u>QUESTIONS OF FACT</u> <u>QUESTIONS OF VALUE</u>

Draw the attention of your class to the bulletin board area and distribute two 3 x 5 inch cards to each pupil.

Ask the pupils to write their names and a factual question on one card and a value question about smoking on the other.

Collect the cards and shuffle them. Then distribute them again in such a way that each pupil receives one card of each type. Have pupils do research to find their answers to the factual questions and give serious thought to the value questions.

Answers should be written on the back side of the card. When answers have been completed students should sign and mount the cards on the appropriate side of the bulletin board with the questions facing out.

At appropriate times have selected students go to the bulletin board and locate the questions they entered. Have them read their questions from the front of the card and the answer given by the respondent on the back of the card to the class.

When the person asking the question and the respondent differ about the correctness of the answer, have them discuss the differences and give each opportunity to prove that his answer or opinion is correct.

D. Variation: Have a medical doctor come to the class to speak about the effects of smoking on the body.

2. GOOD OR BAD? (Grades 3-8)
VALUE: WISE CHOICES FOR GOOD HEALTH

A. Purpose: To help pupils understand that most substances have both good and bad aspects and to encourage them to choose the good.

B. Materials: Bulletin board space. Library resource materials.

C. Procedure: Mount the following caption and outline on your bulletin board:

GOOD OR BAD? MAKE A WISE CHOICE

Items related to your health	Good use	Bad use
drugs		
alcohol		
sweets		
exercise		
sleep		

After you have the caption and organizing divisions on the bulletin board for pupils to see, introduce the idea that many things related to health have both good and bad qualities but that they can be either used for good or bad purposes. For example, drugs can be used to relieve pain and overcome illness but they can also be used to make addicts of people and to even cause harm or death in cases of overdose.

Encourage pupils to find and mount pictures that illustrate good and bad uses of the items listed in the left column or to write comments on 3 x 5 inch cards that explain how the item could be used in either a good or bad way. Such cards should also be mounted in the appropriate section of the bulletin board.

After a sizeable number of entries have been mounted, hold a summarizing discussion on the importance of the wise and good use of all items related to our health and the danger of bad or harmful use of items that of themselves appear to be only good.

3. CLEANLINESS CHART (Grades K-4)
VALUE: CLEANLINESS

A. Purpose: To encourage pupils to develop and apply habits of cleanliness and good grooming.

B. Materials: 3 x 5 inch cards, felt pen.

C. Procedure: Begin by making an individual cleanliness chart for each pupil on a 3 x 5 inch card. This could be made on a duplicated sheet as well and run off. The days of the week should be written across the top of the card with one column being used for each day. The items to be checked should be listed down the left side as shown:

CLEANLINESS CHART OF _____	Monday	Tuesday	Wednesday	Thursday	Friday
Hands and face washed					
Teeth brushed					
Hair combed					
Fingernails trimmed & clean					

Introduce the use of the chart to the children by teaching them the importance of personal cleanliness in good health. Plan a program of "inspections" and record the successful achievement on the pupil's individual record chart.

4. GROWTH FOLDER (Grades K-6)
VALUE: GROWTH AWARENESS

A. Purpose: To help pupils become aware of their growth over the period of a school term.

B. Materials: A folder for each child, a picture of each child taken at the beginning and the ending of the school term.

C. Procedure: At the beginning of the school year, start a folder for each child. Include as many of the following as possible:

    1. A picture of the child at the beginning of the school term.

    2. A chart on which weight and height can be recorded monthly.

    3. Various samples of the pupil's work showing growth in intellectual ability.

4. Notes about the social and emotional growth that occurs as evident from the pupil's behavior patterns.

Hold individual conferences periodically with each pupil to review the growth folders and allow pupils to select materials to include in them. Also hold a concluding conference with each child about the growth and progress throughout the past term and give the folder to the child at that time.

5. HELEN KELLER'S LESSON (Grades 3-6)
VALUE: CARING FOR YOUR EYES

A. Purpose: To help pupils appreciate their ability to see and to care for their eyes.

B. Materials: A copy of the biography or a story about Helen Keller. Research materials on Braille writing and Seeing Eye Dogs.

C. Procedure: Introduce the wonder of the ability to see and read the story of the life of Helen Keller to the class.

Discuss the many ways in which persons who are blinded or have limited vision adjust to this handicap. Follow this discussion by having selected students make reports on Seeing Eye Dogs or the Braille system of writing.

Formulate a set of rules or guidelines for the care of the eyes and help your class in applying them.

D. Variation: Invite a local optometrist to come to speak to your class about eye care.

6. HEALTH SERVANT'S COLLAGE (Grades K-3)
VALUE: APPRECIATION AND RESPECT

A. Purpose: To help children appreciate the work

of the many community health servants who seek their welfare and to build respect for such health servants and the work they do.

B. Materials: Poster paper, a number of old magazines from which pictures may be cut, scissors, paste.

C. Procedure: Discuss the questions, "Who helps me to keep healthy?" and "Who helps me when I'm not?" Use some of the following questions to enable the children to think of some specific examples:

1. Who would help me if I had a toothache?
2. Who would help me if I was in a serious car accident?
3. Who would help me if I broke my leg?
4. Who would help me if........?

To help the pupils gain a clearer understanding of the answers to these and other similar questions, have them make a collage of the pictures of health servants.

Provide each pupil with an old magazine and a pair of scissors. Ask them to find and cut out pictures of people who help others stay healthy or help them when they are not well. Have them arrange and paste the pictures on a sheet of poster paper to form an attractive collage. You may wish to allow the children to search for additonal pictures at home.

When the collages have been completed, provide an opportunity for each pupil to explain how the people pictured on his/her collage help to keep others healthy or help them when they are not well.

Summarize the activity with a discussion that highlights the appreciation and respect we should have for those who help us stay well.

D. Variation: Have someone in the field of health services come to the classroom to explain how he/she was trained for the work to be done and the jobs and satisfactions as well as the problems connected with that particular type of career.

7. JUST SUPPOSE (Grades 3-8)
VALUE: WISE DECISIONS

A. Purpose: To help pupils strengthen their decision making skill in case they find harmful substances.

B. Materials: Pictures of a variety of harmful or potentially dangerous substances such as an unmarked bottle of pills, an unmarked bottle of old medicine, a pack of cigarettes, etc.

C. Procedure: Divide your class into discussion groups of four or five. Have pupils suppose that they are walking home from school with a small group of friends when one of the group notices an unmarked bottle of pills (or other potentially harmful substance.) Just suppose that you pick up the bottle of pills and one of your friends dares you to try one just for fun.

Have each group discuss the situation and formulate the best arguments against experimenting with unknown and potentially harmful substances.

Have reporters from each group present the best arguments of their small group to the class.

D. Variation: Have pupils role play the parts as a form of reporting their arguments to the class.

8. IS IT JUST GOOD OR GOOD FOR YOU? (Grades K-3)
VALUE: PROPER NUTRITION

A. Purpose: To encourage pupils to select and eat foods that are not only good to the taste but also good from the point of view of nutrition.

B. Materials: Pictures of a wide range of food advertisements. Bulletin board space.

C. Procedure: Mount the following caption on your bulletin board:

CHOOSE YOUR FOODS WISELY	
Tastes Good but Is Not Good For You	Tastes Good and Is Good For You Too

Discuss the kinds of foods that members of your class like best. Is the food that we like best always the best for us? What makes a given food really "good"?

Have pupils cut out pictures of various foods from popular magazines and mount these in the proper area on the bulletin board. After a number have been mounted, discuss if each is in the correct place.

D. Variation: Invite the school nutrition expert or the person in charge of planning meals for the school cafeteria to speak to your class about the nutritive qualities of various foods.

9. TRAITS OR HABITS (Grades 2-5)
VALUE: GOOD HABITS

A. Purpose: To convince pupils that habits which

can be changed are more important to a pleasing personality than inherited traits which cannot be changed.

B. Materials: Bulletin board space. A supply of 3 x 5 inch cards.

C. Procedure: Mount the following caption on your bulletin board:

WHICH IS MORE IMPORTANT?	
Inherited Traits (unchangeable)	Personal Habits (changeable)

Call the attention of your class to the bulletin board display that you have started. Discuss the difference between the inherited traits of people such as the color of hair and skin, size, etc. Note with your class that these are generally unchangeable, that is, changing them is generally beyond our normal control. Next consider the column headed, "Personal Habits." Discuss ways in which good habits can make a person likeable and pleasant to be with. Note that since habits are learned, they can be changed or re-learned.

Next distribute several 3 x 5 inch cards to each pupil. Ask them to think of several important qualities that they believe a good friend should have. Ask them to write these qualities on separate cards. Have pupils mount their completed cards on the appropriate side of the bulletin board. (In most cases, most cards will be mounted on the "Good Habits, changeable" side.

Discuss the qualities the pupils listed on their cards together with ways in which we can improve our habits to achieve these desirable qualities.

10. TO LOVE YOUR WORK (Grades 5-8)
VALUE: SATISFACTION

A. Purpose: To make pupils aware of the kinds of satisfactions that persons in various careers get from the particular type of work they do.

B. Materials: Information about various careers and/or persons engaged in various types of work who could be interviewed. Writing paper.

C. Procedure: Discuss the importance of work in the life of grown-ups. Include the many ways in which adults in your community make a living. Note with your class the different situations in which people work, the different things with which they work, etc. Raise the question "What kinds of joys and satisfaction does a person get from doing any kind of work?" Stress the satisfaction pupils can get from doing their school work well.

Note also that persons engaged in different types of work get different types of satisfaction from the work they do. Have pupils do library research about the various careers and the satisfactions persons engaged in them get from their work.

Appoint committees to interview persons in your community who are engaged in different types of work. After they have learned about what these persons do and what they particularly enjoy about their work, have the committee members report their findings to the class.

Conclude the study by having the pupils write a paragraph or theme using this opening sentence as a starter, "I think I would like to be a _____ because _____."

11. WORKING THROUGH ONE'S HOSTILE FEELINGS (Grades K-8)
VALUE: DEALING WITH HOSTILITY

A. Purpose: To provide positive or at least harmless ways for the pupils to work through the hostile feelings they have.

B. Materials: Chalkboard, writing materials.

C. Procedure: Introduce the idea that nearly everyone has hostile feelings at some time or another and we must learn to deal with these feelings of hostility in appropriate ways.

On the chalkboard, write the caption, "THE BEST THING FOR ME TO DO WHEN I AM ANGRY IS..."

Solicit as many appropriate responses from your class as possible and list them on the chalkboard. If pupils do not suggest the following ways, do try to include them:

1. Participate in large muscle activities to expend the excessive energy aroused.
2. Discussing the problem with an adult friend and asking that person's advice.
3. Analyze the reasons why you are angry and consider ways in which the problem can be resolved calmly.
4. Consider the possibility of just being by yourself until the initial sensation of anger has passed.
5. Be careful not to hurt yourself or others at a time of anger.

As pupils suggest various responses, add them to the chalkboard list.

Next hold a class discussion to help pupils evaluate the different types of responses listed and determine which are most appropriate.

Next have pupils copy the list in the order that they feel is most appropriate for them personally. Encourage them to follow the list to work out their hostilities when the need arises.

12. HOW DO YOU FEEL TODAY? (Grades 3-7)
VALUE: BUILDING FRIENDSHIPS

A. Purpose: To help pupils realize that their own behavior affects the way others behave toward them.

B. Materials: A bulletin board display of people's faces showing all types of moods, e.g. happy faces, grumpy faces, etc., chart paper, felt pens.

C. Procedure: During the early part of a school day call the attention of your class to your bulletin board display. Ask them to look at one picture and tell how the person in the picture was feeling or what attitude the person was showing on his face. Follow this same procedure with several other pictures and record the reaction of the pupils on a chart like that shown below:

Feeling or Attitude shown on the face	Would you enjoy being with a person when he/she felt that way?

Next have each pupil pick out one of the attitudes and write it on a small piece of paper with his/her name and place the paper in a box on your desk.

Ask the pupils not to tell anyone else which attitude or feeling they wrote on the paper. Instead have them act it out for most of the school day.

Near the end of the day, move to the next step in the learning activity by having the pupils decide which attitude or feeling was acted out by one another.

After the feelings and attitudes have been noted, which they thought each child portrayed, check with the slips of paper in the box to see if they were identified correctly.

Summarize by means of the following discussion questions:

    1. If a person acted grumpy all day long, did that person enjoy the role? Did he/she attract or lose friends?

    2. If a person acted happy and friendly all day long, did that person enjoy the role? Did he/she attract or lose friends?

Help the class conclude that one can attract and hold friends more readily by being cheerful than by being grumpy.

13. RITES OF PASSAGE (Grades 6-8)
VALUE: REACHING MATURITY

A. Purpose: To help pupils realize that "growing up" provides both added responsibilities and privileges.

B. Materials: Information about the "Rites of Passage" which allow young people of various cultures or tribes to assume the rights and responsibilities of adulthood.

C. Procedure: Introduce the idea of growing up at a time when students complain about not being allowed enough privileges. Emphasize that the problem of growing up is common to young people in many cultures.

Divide the class into groups to do research about the "Rites of Passage" of various Indian tribes or people of other cultures. Note how young people had to prove their adulthood.

Next put the following chart on the chalkboard.

GROWING UP BRINGS...

ADDED PRIVILEGES	ADDED RESPONSIBILITIES

Solicit items from your class to complete the chart. Include such items as the following:

Get driver's license	Learn to drive with care
Choose own clothes	Choose clothes wisely

Summarize the activity by pointing out that adults will increase the amount of independence they give to young people in proportion to the degree that the young people accept the responsibilities and privileges that such increased independence requires.

D. Variation: Divide your class into a number of committees and have them interview selected adults to learn what they consider to be the characteristics of grown-up behavior. Have the committees formulate a series of questions such as the following to use in their interviews:

What kinds of things do young people do today that make you think of them as being irresponsible or immature?

What kinds of things should young people do to prove to you that they are responsible and grown-up?

When you were our age, what did the "older

generation" expect of you as you were growing up?

What suggestions do you have to help us to be accepted as mature and responsible adults?

Have the class add other questions that are especially important to them.

After the committees have completed their interviews, hold a concluding discussion on ways in which young people could prove their ability to assume responsibility.

SECTION FIVE

VALUES RELATED TO AUTHORITY AND GOVERNMENT

Having proper attitudes toward authority in the home and school as well as toward representatives of all levels of civil government is an important aspect of good citizenship. The activities in this section provide opportunity to develop the values upon which these attitudes are founded.

1. WOULD YOU RIDE WITH PAUL REVERE?
(Grades 6-8)

VALUE: PATRIOTISM

A. Purpose: To help pupils realize that patriotism requires courage.

B. Materials: A copy of the familiar poem, "Paul Revere's Ride" by Henry W. Longfellow. Writing paper and pencils.

C. Procedure: Read the poem, "Paul Revere's Ride" to your class. Have the class members imagine that they were with Paul Revere waiting on the shore for the signal light telling that the British were coming. Hold a class discussion about the poem using the following questions to begin:

1. What feelings did you have as you first saw the light of the lanterns in the church tower?

2. Were you afraid as you raced on horseback to spread the alarm "through every Middlesex village and farm"?

3. What risk were you taking? Why were you willing to take those risks?

Next have the pupils write a creative story about the experience including how they felt while riding with Paul Revere and why they felt that way. Have pupils share the stories they have written. Conclude the lesson by discussing what our patriotism requires of us today.

D. Variation: Rather than reading and having the pupils listen to the poem, if it is included in their literature books, ask the class to read it for themselves and assign a group of students the task of enacting the poem as a play.

2. OVERTIME PARKING (Grades 6-8)
VALUE: PROMPTNESS

A. Purpose: To teach pupils that being late can be costly.

B. Materials: Access to information about parking meters from officials in a city traffic control department.

C. Procedure: Appoint a committee to do research on the topic of parking meters in your city. Have the class formulate a list of questions such as the following for the committee to use:

1. How many meters does the city have placed?
2. How do they decide where they should be?
3. How much money does the city take in from them each year?
4. How is the money collected?
5. What are the advantages of parking meters?
6. How many police officers are employed to issue tickets to parking meter violators?
7. How large is the fine for overtime parking?
8. How does the general public feel about the use of parking meters?

After an appropriate list of questions has been agreed upon, have the committee make an appointment and interview traffic department officials and report to the class the information they have gathered.

Discuss the reasons why people fail to return to their cars on time and the high cost of not doing so promptly. In what other ways is not being prompt costly?

3. LIKE THE PIECES OF A JIGSAW PUZZLE
(Grades 3-6)
VALUE: RESPONSIBILITY

A. Purpose: To help pupils realize that rights and responsibilities go together.

B. Materials: A supply of cardboard rectangles about 3 x 5 inches in size. Scissors and bulletin board space.

C. Procedure: As the background for this activity mount the caption, "THEY FIT TOGETHER", on a bulletin board space.

Next cut out a piece of cardboard about 12 x 16 inches in size. Print the word, "RIGHTS" on the left half and "RESPONSIBILITIES" on the right half. Then cut the card into two pieces using cutting style like that between two pieces of a jigsaw puzzle. Next mount the two pieces under the caption on the bulletin board so it would appear something like the arrangement shown below:

THEY FIT TOGETHER

Discuss with your class what kinds of rights they enjoy. Make a list of these on the chalkboard in one column. Then give each member of the class a piece of cardboard about 3 x 5 inches in size. Ask them to pick out one of the "rights" from the list or select another they think important and write it on the left side of their card. Then have them write a related responsibility on the right side of the card. Next ask them to cut the card into two pieces using their own original jigsaw type of design so the two halves will fit only with one another. An example would be the right to vote on the left side and the responsibility to study the qualifications of candidates and the importance of issues so one can vote wisely on the right side.

After all cards have been prepared and cut, use an empty box to collect them, shake the box gently to thoroughly mix the pieces and allow students to match them up at a learning center table as a spare time activity.

When all students have had an opportunity to match the card parts at the table, mount all the matched pieces on the bulletin board around the original large-sized display set and hold a discussion about how rights and responsibilities fit together.

D. Variation: Have the pupils bring an old jigsaw puzzle to school and assemble it with the blank backside up. Next have pupils think of something that they think is a "right". Some pupil may suggest that having recess at school is a right. Ask pupils to write this "right" on the back of one piece. Next ask what responsibilities go with this "right". Someone may suggest "Good behavior on the playground". This responsibility should be written on the jigsaw puzzle piece that connects to the right to go out to recess. After all the pieces of the puzzle have either a right or a responsibility written on the back, break up the puzzle and use spare time to reassemble them by joining the rights and responsibilities.

4. IS FREEDOM OF SPEECH REALLY FREE? (Grades 2-6)
VALUE: FREEDOM

A. Purpose: To help pupils realize that with the privilege of freedom of speech comes the responsibility to use it wisely.

B. Materials: A copy of the First Amendment to the United States Constitution. Chart paper and felt pen.

C. Procedure: Read the First Amendment to the U.S. Constitution to the class and point out to them how the U.S. government has guaranteed the right of the freedom of speech to its citizens. Next discuss ways in which people could abuse or misuse this right such as by doing the following:

1. Shouting, "Fire, Fire!" in a very crowded building such as a public auditorium when there was no fire just to cause people to panic.
2. Saying false or unkind things about others.
3. Using vulgar or irreverent language.

Ask the class to provide other examples and discuss why the freedom of speech we enjoy gives us added responsibility to use that freedom wisely.

Use the chart paper and felt pen to formulate a set of "Rules for the Use of our Freedom of Speech" with the help of the class.

Display the chart in a prominent place in the classroom to encourage pupils to observe the rules agreed upon.

5. RIGHTING WRONGS (Grades 4-8)
VALUE: JUSTICE

A. Purpose: To encourage pupils to be concerned about injustice and interested in promoting justice.

B. Materials: A number of examples of "wrongs" or "injustices" either from general newspaper stories or from the life experiences of your pupils.

C. Procedure: Discuss the idea of justice with your class. Use the following questions to begin the discussion:
1. What is justice?
2. Have you ever been treated unjustly? How did you feel?
3. Have you ever wanted to right a wrong in your school, your community or society at large?

Use the newspaper stories or experiences the pupils are aware of to make a list of "wrongs." Select one of these that seems to be of prime concern to the members of your class at this point in time and develop a number of alternative ways in which the wrong could be removed or corrected.

Have the class establish a priority order of the most appropriate and effective ways to follow in order to achieve the justice desired. Include such things as writing to lawmakers or other public officials.

After the class has attempted to implement the selected plan of action, evaluate the results.

6. PREAMBLE STUDY (Grades 6-8)
VALUE: PATRIOTISM

A. Purpose: To develop a sense of patriotism and appreciation for our government through a study of its goals as stated in the Preamble to the U.S. Constitution.

B. Materials: Bulletin board space. A copy of the Preamble of the U.S. Constitution. Available old magazines from which pictures can be cut.

C. Procedure: Arrange a bulletin board display of the Preamble of the U.S. Constitution under the caption:

THE GOALS OF OUR GOVERNMENT

"We the people of the United States, in order to form a more perfect union, establish justice, insure domestic tranquillity, provide for the common defense, promote the general welfare, and secure the blessings of liberty to ourselves and our posterity, do ordain and establish this Constitution for the United States of America."

Strengthen the Union	Establish Justice	Insure Domestic Tranquillity
Common Defense	General Welfare	Secure Liberty

In the space immediately underneath the preamble, provide space or a section for each goal.

Lead a class discussion on the meaning of the terms and ask pupils to cut pictures out of old magazines that would illustrate how the government seeks to achieve these goals.

After a sizeable number of pictures have been mounted in each of the sections, ask pupils to explain how the pictures they selected help to illustrate the section heading.

Conclude the activity with a general discussion about the importance of government using the

following questions as a discussion guide:
1. Why is the government necessary?
2. Are the goals of our government as listed in the Preamble good goals?
3. In what ways does our government serve the people of our country?
4. In what ways can we help our government?

7. A PLEDGE IS A PROMISE (Grades 1-4)
VALUE: GOOD CITIZENSHIP

A. Purpose: To help pupils understand the promise they make when they pledge allegiance to the flag.

B. Materials: A United States flag, a copy of the Pledge of Allegiance, bulletin board space, yarn, felt pens, poster paper, magazine pictures.

C. Procedure: After the class has recited the Pledge of Allegiance to the flag, spend some time discussing the meaning of the promise they have just made. Include the significance of placing the right hand (as symbol of one's skill and effort) over the heart (as a symbol of one's life) while the pledge is made.

Mount a copy of the Pledge of Allegiance near the center of the bulletin board space under the caption shown below:

A PLEDGE IS A PROMISE

Use the poster paper and felt pen to explain the terms in the pledge which pupils may have difficulty understanding as follows:

pledge -- a promise
United States of America -- a map of our country or

a picture of the national capitol

  republic -- a form of government where the people elect their government officials
    indivisible -- united, not divided
    liberty -- freedom within the law
    justice -- equal treatment in the courts

To represent "all" in the pledge, you could use a picture of people representing a wide variety of the segments of our American society.

Use the yarn to connect the pictures or placards to the appropriate word in the pledge.

Conclude the learning activity by discussing the meaning of the terms and the importance of loyalty and good citizenship.

D. Variation: Relate the study of the Pledge of Allegiance as a promise to a more general consideration of the nature of promises such as promises we make to one another, promises we make to parents, promises politicians make to gain votes, etc. Include a discussion of why promises should be kept so others will continue to trust us.

8. WHEN OTHERS ARE WATCHING (Grades 4-8)
VALUE: SINCERITY

A. Purpose: To help pupils realize we must obey authority not just when we are being watched but all the time.

B. Materials: Paper ballots.

C. Procedure: Explain to the class that people sometimes do what is right only when others are watching. Write a few examples on the chalkboard such as:

1. A driver who obeys the speed limit only when a police car is following him.

2. A person who crosses the street in the crosswalk only when an officer is near.

Discuss with the class how being obedient to the laws only because of fear of punishment shows that one is not sincere in trying to do what is right.

Next pass out the ballots and ask the class to vote "Yes" if they think their class as a whole is sincere in obeying the rules even when the teacher is out of the room. Ask them to vote "No" if they think the class is generally obedient only when the teacher is present.

Collect and tally the votes. Discuss the results by pointing out that real obedience is sincere. It doesn't depend upon the threat of punishment but rather is motivated by the desire to do what is right.

D. Variation: Have pupils make a study of police strategies used to catch lawbreakers. Discuss why it is necessary for police to hide their cars or use radar to catch motorists during unsuspecting moments. What does this tell us about how sincere people are about obeying the law? Discuss how sincerity can be strengthened.

9. IS IT FIT TO EAT? (Grades 5-8)
VALUE: PURE FOOD

A. Purpose: To make pupils aware of the many rules and regulations that guard the purity of our food.

B. Materials: Address of the National Food and Drug Administration as follows:

Food and Drug Administration
U.S. Dept. of Health, Education & Welfare
7915 Eastern Avenue
Washington, D.C. 20204

The address of local Health Department offices, letter writing materials.

C. Procedure: When your students are studying foods in health class, discuss the concept of food purity using the following questions as discussion starters:

1. How are food products such as fruits and vegetables washed and prepared for use, canning or shipment to food stores?

2. How are meat products inspected and kept clean from farm to market?

3. What cleanliness standards must be met by restaurants as they prepare foods?

Follow the discussion of these questions with a consideration of how food is kept pure when it is raised and/or prepared at home.

Have pupils write to the Food and Drug Administration to obtain copies of laws that protect the purity of food. Contact a local food establishment to ask how they meet the laws governing food purity.

Conclude the learning activity by pointing out why the many laws that guard the purity of our food are necessary.

D. Variation: Contact the local health department offices and invite an official who is responsible for inspecting local food establishments to speak to your class about both the rules that are to be enforced and the kinds of violations that are most common.

10. PENALTIES FOR DRUG ABUSE (Grades 6-8)
VALUE: AVOIDING PENALTY

A. Purpose: To help pupils realize that those who break drug control laws may be subjected to severe penalties.

B. Materials: Access to library research materials and information on drug control laws and the penalties for their violation.

C. Procedure: Discuss the idea of penalties for the breaking of laws. Begin the discussion by considering the following questions with your class:

1. What kinds of penalties do parents often enforce if children disobey the rules of the home?
2. What kinds of penalties do teachers and other school officials enforce if students disobey the rules of the school?
3. Why do all segments of society (city, state, nation, club, team, etc.) have rules for the way they conduct their affairs?
4. Would people pay attention to rules if there were no penalties for breaking them? Why or why not?

Move the general discussion of penalties for breaking rules or laws to the more specific area of laws that control the abuse of drugs. Have pupils do research on the topic to discover what laws there are to control the distribution as well as the penalties specified for their violation. Include a study of any current newspaper items on the topic. Ask the pupils to report their findings to the class.

Conclude the learning activity by noting that more severe penalties are given when a law that governs the misuse of a more dangerous drug is violated. Highlight the concept that one avoids penalties by obeying the law and that the purpose of laws is for the common good.

11. WHAT IS A LAW? (Grades 3-6)
VALUE: UNDERSTANDING LAWS

A. Purpose: To help pupils understand what laws are and why they are useful.

B. Materials: A copy of several laws that govern local conditions such as speed, parking, hunting, fishing, etc.

C. Procedure: Have the class imagine that you and your family and they with their families were all going to move to a beautiful uninhabited island in the South Seas. You can have the class discuss what the island is like before you arrive.

As your ship approaches the island, a meeting is called with the class members each serving as the representatives of their families and a discussion is held about how the group will govern itself on the island.

After a number of "laws" have been proposed and adopted, move the class discussion to a consideration of what laws are and why they are both necessary and useful.

Refer to a number of local laws by completing a chart similar to the following on the chalkboard:

Local law	Reason why law is useful or necessary

Conclude the learning activity by pointing out the responsibility of all citizens to obey the laws and if the laws are bad or inadequate to work for better laws.

12. MAKE A GRAPH (Grades 6-8)
VALUE: CONTROLLING CRIME

A. Purpose: To help pupils visualize the problem of controlling crime.

B. Materials: Graph paper. Statistics on crime growth. Samples of bar, circle and broken line graphs.

C. Procedure: Present the graphs that you have and note with your class how a graph gives a quick and dynamic picture of the facts.

Next announce an "optional" project for students to do during any free time they may have. Have them select one of the following topics related to crime control:

1. The cost of crime to business each year since 1960.
2. The number of automobile accidents caused by drunken drivers since 1960.
3. The number of crimes causing personal injury to others each year since 1960.
4. Some other aspect of the crime problem....

Ask pupils to gather statistics on the crime problem selected and make a graph of the information gathered.

Have students present their graphs to the class. Also ask them to present their suggestions for controlling the type of crime they have researched and illustrated.

13. ON TRIAL (Grades 6-8)
VALUE: JUSTICE

A. Purpose: To help pupils understand the need for justice in dealing with wrongdoers.

B. Materials: Access to a local court so the class can observe a trial in progress. Library reference material.

C. Procedure: After making a study of the court process and observing a trial in action, set up a "court" in your classroom complete with judge, jury and lawyers for prosecution and defense.

When a student is suspected of violating a school or classroom rule, have the "case" presented to the "court" for trial. Be sure that all of the "due processes" of law to protect the innocent and bringing the guilty to justice are followed.

14. NOT LIKE LIGHTNING (Grades 4-8)
VALUE: POWER NEEDS CONTROL

A. Purpose: To help pupils realize that uncontrolled power may be dangerous.

B. Materials: Pictures of lightning and power lines to a city. References relating to the power and destructive nature of lightning.

C. Procedure: Show the pictures of lightning flashes to the class. Note with them its destructive power:

1. It causes forest fires.
2. It may kill animals or persons.
3. It may destroy buildings.

Next show the pictures of the high-power lines through which electrical power flows in well-controlled ways to run factories and light homes.

Compare the destructive forces of electrical power that is uncontrolled and the useful force of controlled electricity.

Move the discussion to the more general topic of how all power that is uncontrolled can become

harmful even though it has much potential for good when controlled. Use such examples as the following:
- Destructive floods and hydroelectric plants
- Windmills and tornadoes
- Horses running in a wild runaway and pulling together
- A car out of control and one in control

Summarize the activity by pointing out that any power when uncontrolled can become destructive.

D. Variation: Have pupils prepare posters illustrating safety rules to observe during a thunder and lightning storm.

15. RIGHT, WRONG OR MAYBE (Grades 5-8)
VALUE: EQUAL JUSTICE

A. Purpose: To help pupils realize that while many actions can readily be judged as clearly right or clearly wrong, others are not so easily decided.

B. Materials: Daily newspapers and bulletin board space.

C. Procedure: Mount the following caption on your bulletin board:

YOU BE THE JUDGE

Right   ??????????   Wrong

Begin the learning activity by reviewing several newspaper items with your class. First read a clipping that illustrates some event that is clearly right and mount it on the bulletin board in the "Right" column. Next read an item that clearly illustrates something that was wrong to do and mount it in the "Wrong" column.

Next read a few clippings that illustrate happenings which may be considered right by some persons and wrong by others and mount them in the middle column under the question marks.

Have pupils bring clippings to school and mount them in the appropriate column. After several days have gone by and a sizeable number of clippings have been put up, hold a class discussion about the reasons why some people may consider the same event right while others may consider it wrong.

Lead the discussion to the obvious need that our nation has for laws which set a common standard for a judge in our courts to use in providing equal justice for all.

16. CAMPAIGN PROMISES (Grades 5-8)
VALUE: RESPONSIBLE PROMISES

A. Purpose: To help pupils distinguish between responsible and irresponsible promises.

B. Materials: A variety of newspaper stories, election brochures and candidate flyers dealing with election campaign promises. Bulletin board space and 3 x 5 inch cards.

C. Procedure: Use this learning activity at a time when a national or local election is being held.

Mount the following caption on your bulletin board:

CAMPAIGN PROMISES

RESPONSIBLE   IRRESPONSIBLE

As the election campaign progresses have pupils

bring news stories and campaign literature, flyers, etc., to class. Have the pupils read the material carefully and decide whether the promises made are responsible or irresponsible and mount the articles on the appropriate side of the bulletin board. Discuss with your class what the difference is between being responsible or irresponsible in the many promises we make.

Summarize the activity by noting with your class how important making responsible promises is in establishing trust.

17. SIMULATING SIGNING THE DECLARATION OF INDEPENDENCE (Grades 5-8)
VALUE: FREEDOM

A. Purpose: To have pupils experience the commitment to freedom made by the signers of the Declaration of Independence.

B. Materials: A signed copy and an unsigned replica of the Declaration of Independence. Costumes of colonial days. Quill pen and ink. Research materials covering the American Revolutionary Period in U. S. history.

C. Procedure: Initiate this learning activity by displaying a copy of the Declaration of Independence. Note especially with your class the final paragraph which reads as follows:

We, therefore, the Representatives of the United States of America, in General Congress, assembled, appealing to the Supreme Judge of the world for the rectitude of our intentions, do, in the Name, and by the Authority of the good people of these Colonies, solemnly publish and declare, that these United Colonies are, and of Right ought to be FREE and INDEPENDENT STATES: that they are Absolved from all Allegiance to the British Crown, and that all political connection between them and the State of Great Britain, is and ought to be totally dissolved; and that as Free and Independent States, they have full Power to levy War, conclude Peace, contract Alliances, establish Commerce, and to do all other Acts and Things which independent States may of right do. And for the support of this Declaration, with a firm reliance on the protection of divine Providence, we mutually pledge to each other our Lives, our fortunes and our sacred Honor.

Discuss what the signers of the Declaration of Independence were willing to risk for freedom. Have a committee do research about how the lives of the men who signed the Declaration were affected by their commitment to freedom. Have the class note the courage it must have taken to be a signer.

Next have pupils dress up in costumes similar to the clothes worn at the time of the American Revolution and role play the signing of the Declaration of Independence.

D. Variation: Have the pupils prepare and sign a Declaration of Human Rights or Freedom that would be appropriate in today's world.

18. WHO MADE THE RULES? (Grades 4-8)
VALUE: RESPECTING AUTHORITY
  A. Purpose: To help pupils relate the rules they

are expected to obey to the authority by which they were made.

B. Materials: Writing materials.

C. Procedure: Have pupils make a list of all the rules they are expected to obey.

Next discuss the various "authorities" that have made the rules and establish a key or code similar to the one shown below:

    H -- Home
    S -- School
    G -- Civil Government

These broad categories can be divided further to distinguish between father and mother in the home, teacher, principal, bus driver, librarian, etc. in the school; fire department, police department, city, state, federal, etc., in the system of civil government. If you wish, you can add these to the coding system.

Ask the pupils to then place a code letter in front of each of the rules they have listed to indicate which "authority" they are obeying when they obey the rule.

Discuss the nature of the penalty that would result if any of the rules listed were violated.

D. Variation: Discuss what we should do or what process we should follow if we feel a law is unjust. Note the difference between the formal way we obey the laws of civil government and the way we show love to our parents when we do what they ask us to do.

SECTION SIX

VALUES RELATED TO PROPERTY

Public property and the property of others should be treated with as much care as if it were one's own. The activities in this section will encourage pupils to develop values upon which they can build proper attitudes toward all property

1. FOR SALE (Grades 5-8)
VALUE: HONESTY

A. Purpose: To help strengthen the pupils' sense of the need for honesty in business transactions.

B. Materials: The classified advertisement section of your local newspaper including a variety of items for sale. Chart paper and felt pen.

C. Procedure: Review the various kinds of things for sale in the classified ads of your local newspaper. Discuss with your class the reasons why the person placing the ad may wish to sell the items listed for sale. Include in your discussion a consideration of the advantages and disadvantages of purchasing used rather than new merchandise. Use a few examples from the newspaper ads to complete a chart similar to that shown below on your chart paper:

Item for sale	Possible reasons for selling	Possible problems if purchased in used condition

Next raise the question of whether or not you should tell the buyer what is wrong with the item you had advertised and are trying to sell.

Discuss the importance of honesty when one advertises something for sale or sells something to someone else.

D. Variation: Have members of your class role play situations such as the following:

1. A boy who is going to sell his old bicycle because he wishes to buy a new one. Another boy comes to see it. They talk about the bicycle before the sale is made.

2. A girl wishes to sell her record player. An interested person comes to inquire about it before purchasing it.

3. A man has his car advertised for sale. Another man comes to see it and to talk to him before purchasing it.

4. Select a few ads from the local newspaper and role play the seller and purchaser of each.

Conclude the class session by discussing the importance of honesty in business transactions.

2. IF I HAD A MILLION DOLLARS (Grades 4-7)
VALUE: STEWARDSHIP

A. Purpose: To have pupils realize that the ownership of property carries with it an obligation to use it wisely.

B. Materials: A daily newspaper.

C. Procedure: Begin the lesson by scanning the newspaper in front of your class. Share with them some of the major items in the news such as tensions between nations on the international scene and tragedies of fire, flood and other more local concerns.

Next turn to a wide range of advertisements including those of grocery and hardware stores as well as automobile and real estate agencies.

Ask the class members to imagine they had each suddenly received one million dollars. Have them write a creative story on how they would use it in connection with what you had just noted with them from the newspaper.

Have various volunteers read their papers to the class. Follow this with a discussion about the opportunities to do good to others that would be open to someone who actually received a million dollars. Then move to a discussion about the responsibilities that go with wealth or ownership of any amount of property whether the amount is large or small.

D. Variation: Instead of having pupils write a creative story in response to the use of property, have them make a collage in art class of good things they could do for others if they had a million dollars.

3. PUT IT IN THE BANK (Grades 2-6)
VALUE: SAVING/THRIFT

A. Purpose: To encourage pupils to develop the habit of saving a portion of the money they earn rather than spending all of it as or even before it is earned.

B. Materials: A savings account book and information about savings accounts from your local bank. Advertisements from a newspaper showing amounts of interest money can earn if placed in the bank.

C. Procedure: Solicit from the class some ideas on the ways they receive or can earn money. Some may receive regular allowances from their parents; other may earn money by doing odd jobs for their parents or neighbors; by delivering papers or by baby-sitting. During the summer months some students may mow lawns, pick fruit or hold other jobs.

Note with them that children as well as adults may receive more money at some times than at others. For example, if a farmer sold his grain crop in the fall when it was harvested and spent all the money he received at that time, he would have a real money problem the rest of the year. Saving is one way of helping you distribute your income so that you will have some money to spend at a later time when you need something but don't have an income.

Use the savings account book to teach pupils how a savings account works. Discuss the concept of interest as money that the bank pays you for the use of your money.

D. Variation: Plan a field trip to a local bank and arrange to have a bank representative speak to the students about how savings accounts work, how the vault operates, etc.

4. ANALYZE ADVERTISING (Grades 5-8)
VALUE: DISCERNMENT

A. Purpose: To encourage pupils to look carefully at advertisements in common magazines to determine the basis for their appeal.

B. Materials: A number of magazines from which advertisements could be cut.

C. Procedure: Have pupils collect advertisements that are appealing. Include ads about cigarettes, hair shampoo, cold remedies, relaxing medications, liquor, etc.

Next have pupils note why the advertisements are appealing. Try to classify them according to the basis for their appeal such as color use, pleasure or relaxation, relief from pain or anxiety, freedom, nature, manliness, womanly beauty, etc.

Have pupils determine if the basis for appeal has anything to do with the product being advertised. For example, will the smoking of a given brand of cigarettes lead one to a greater enjoyment of mountain streams? Or, will taking a given type of product to relieve a headache remove the problem that caused it?

Have each child select an advertisement and explain to the class why it appealed to him/her. Also have the child try to discern if the message it gives is honest. Conclude the discussion by summarizing the need to exercise discernment in the way one reacts to advertisements.

5. A BROKEN WINDOW (Grades 5-8)
VALUE: REDUCING VANDALISM

A. Purpose: To help pupils realize the great cost to society of windows broken on purpose.

B. Materials: Access to records of a local school system and a local glass replacement company.

C. Procedure: Select an occasion when a window has been broken "anonymously" in the school or in one of the homes or cars of your pupils. Decide with your class to investigate the number of windows replaced and the cost of glass replacement in your school and neighboring school district during a one year period. Compare the total with the amount spent for athletic equipment, for library materials, film rentals or some other part of the school budget. Note how many other worthwhile things could be purchased if no windows had been broken.

Appoint a committee of the class to visit a glass company to obtain the prices on glass replacement. Have pupils measure various windows in the school and their homes so they have definite sizes about which to inquire. The committee could use the prices obtained to figure out what it would cost to replace all of the windows in the school.

Appoint another committee to visit a local automobile glass replacement company. Have them investigate what it would cost to replace the windshield in each of their family cars as well as in other makes and models. Have the committee inquire about the number of broken car windows replaced by the company that were caused by accidents compared to the number broken through vandalism.

Summarize the activity by discussing the cost of broken windows to private property owners and to taxpayers. Discuss how much good the money could do if it were spent in more worthwhile ways.

6. SPRAY PAINT (Grades 6-8)
VALUE: CARE OF PUBLIC PROPERTY

A. Purpose: To help pupils realize the destructive nature of spray painting.

B. Materials: A spray paint can, various types of paint removers, a board to be sprayed.

C. Procedure: Ask pupils if they have seen any public building, bridges, park benches, etc., defaced by spray paint. Note with your class how this destroys the appearance of buildings or whatever was maliciously spray painted.

Have pupils make a neighborhood survey to note where such paint had been applied. Also note the kinds of words applied such as the names of persons or schools. Discuss how this reflects negatively on that person or school.

Show the destructive nature of spray painting by spraying a board and allowing it to dry. Next give the students the opportunity to try to wipe it off with various cleaners or paint removers. Have pupils notice both how difficult it is to remove paint once it has dried and how attempting to do so tends to destroy the original paint.

D. Variation: Have pupils contact the maintenance departments of the city or of the state park departments to determine the cost in time and materials to cover the destructive spray painting done in your area.

7. FINDERS KEEPERS (Grades 4-7)
VALUE: HONESTY

A. Purpose: To encourage pupils to practice honesty by returning any item they find to its rightful owner.

B. Materials: A number of old wallets.

C. Procedure: Describe the following situation to your class: Two pupils are riding home from school on a city bus (or walking home on the sidewalk) when they find a wallet with $50 and the identification of the owner in it.

Divide your class into pairs or teams. Have one pupil on each team be anxious to return the billfold to its owner while the other pupil advises him/her to keep it. After a five minute period of discussion have the pupils exchange roles and continue the discussion.

Summarize the discussion by highlighting the best reason each team formulated for returning the wallet to its owner.

Conduct an experiment using the old wallets. Have selected pupils put an identification card including name, address, phone number, etc., plus an important paper or two and, if possible, a small amount of money. Have them "lose" the old wallets "on purpose". Make a chart of who the "owner" of each wallet is, description of each wallet and its contents, and where it was officially "lost".

Record the time and date when the wallets are returned and by whom they were found. Ask the persons who return the wallets why they did so rather than keep the money for themselves.

Conclude the lesson by having members of your class write "Thank You" letters to the persons who returned the wallets.

D. Variation: In a language arts class have the student write a newspaper article on the importance of honesty. Include the results of your experiment with the lost wallets and their return. You may wish to have the best articles submitted to the school or local newspaper for possible publication.

8. CHOOSING THE RIGHT TOOL (Grades 2-6)
VALUE: CHOOSING APPROPRIATELY

A. Purpose: To help pupils appreciate the wide variety of tools available today and increase their ability to choose the right tool for a given task.

B. Materials: A number of mail-order catalogs from which pictures can be cut. Bulletin board space. 3 x 5 inch cards.

C. Procedure: Mount the caption "CHOOSE THE RIGHT TOOL" on the bulletin board. Then present the ideas of the many types of tools available for purchase and use today.

Turn to the mail-order catalog and show the many varieties of tools available. Write the sentence, "TO _____ USE A _____" on the chalkboard.

Then show your class as you copy this on a 3 x 5 inch card. Next fill in the words "drive in a nail" in the first blank. Then cut a picture of a hammer out of the catalog and paste it on the card in the space as shown below:

Then pin the card on the bulletin board as a sample of one tool and what it is used for.

Challenge the pupils to make a similar card for each tool they can find. In each case they should tell what the use of the tool is and supply a picture of it.

After pupils have had the opportunity to use both the catalogs available in class and other sources of pictures of tools such as magazines, etc., in their homes, note the wide range of tools pictured.

Summarize the activity by counting the number of different tools the class was able to find and the uses of each. Note with your pupils how the use of tools makes work easier.

D. Variation: Arrange for a display of tools and have the shop teacher or a local carpenter demonstrate their use.

9. WORKAHOLICS (Grades 5-8)
VALUE: CONTENTMENT

A. Purpose: To help pupils realize that contentment can bring happiness.

B. Materials: Newspaper ad of a store that is remodeling and enlarging.

C. Procedure: Show the newspaper ad to your class and ask what advantages the remodeling and enlarging of the store will have for the customers and for the company.

Next discuss the idea of companies that grow bigger and bigger and compare this to the compelling drive an individual person may have to earn more and more. Use the following questions as discussion starters:

    1. Is it good for a person to want to be successful and be willing to work hard to achieve success? Why or why not?

    2. When does the drive to be successful become a negative rather than a positive force?

    3. When is it that a person can be called a "workaholic"?

    4. What does contentment mean?

    5. How can one balance ambition with contentment?

Conclude the lesson by having pupils write a short theme in which they compare the life styles of persons who--

    1. Have no ambition.
    2. Have too much ambition.
    3. Balance ambition with contentment.

10. WHEN YOU BORROW SOMETHING (Grades 2-8)
    VALUE: RETURNING BORROWED ITEMS

A. Purpose: To teach pupils how to borrow and return things properly.

B. Materials: Poster paper, felt pen.

C. Procedure: Ask your class if anyone has ever borrowed something from them and either failed to return it or returned it in a damaged condition. How did they feel when this happened?

Does anyone recall borrowing something from someone and then finding that you lost or broke the item you borrowed before you could return it?

On a sheet of poster paper, have your class make a list of rules for borrowing. Include some of the following together with those that the class suggests:

1. Always ask permission of the owner before you borrow something.
2. Agree on when the item is to be returned.
3. Take extra care of items borrowed.
4. Return the item in as good condition as it was when you borrowed it.
5. If the item borrowed is lost or broken, it should be replaced.

After the poster has been completed, hang it in an obvious place in the classroom or school.

D. Variation: Write the following words in chart form on the chalkboard:

Borrow	Rent	Buy

Have the class tell the difference between the three terms. Next solicit from the class a list of items they or their family use such as a house, a car, a bicycle, a special tool, clothing, food, etc. Write the items in an appropriate column on the chart.

Note that some items could appear in more than one column, e.g., a house may be rented or bought. Discuss with your class the advantages and disadvantages of each.

11. WHAT CAN I DO WITH MONEY? (Grades 4-7)
VALUE: USING MONEY WISELY

A. Purpose: To help pupils realize that there are three chief ways to use money.

B. Materials: Poster paper, felt pen.

C. Procedure: Ask your class what the chief uses of money are. Try to lead the class to suggest the headings to the following columns. Write them on the chalkboard in the form of a chart.

HOW WE CAN USE MONEY		
You can SAVE money	You can GIVE money away	You can SPEND money
Why is it wise to save some money?	Why should you use some of your money to give away?	What are some of the things one needs to spend money for?
Where is the best place to save it?	What kinds of projects should you support?	What are some of the things we must consider if we are to do so wisely?

Use the questions shown in each of the columns above to clinch ideas about each of the three ways in which money can be used.

Conclude the exercise by emphasizing the need to develop habits of using money wisely.

12. WISE CONSUMERS (Grades 4-8)
VALUE: CHOOSING PURCHASES WISELY

A. Purpose: To provide opportunity for pupils to think about and make judgments regarding the things they buy.

B. Materials: Chalkboard space and old newspaper advertisements.

C. Procedure: With your class, make a list of various representative groups in our society in one column on the chalkboard and a list of some of their needs in another. A few examples are listed below:

PERSONS	NEEDS	WISEST CHOICES
A pupil about to start school at the beginning of the fall term		
A young person about to enter college		
A young couple about to be married		
A family planning a camping trip		

Have pupils suggest things that persons in the left column would likely need and list these needs in the middle column. Try to find costs of the articles "needed" in newspaper advertisements or have committees of pupils gather information about costs from stores.

Next discuss what the wisest choices would be. Use questions like the following to start the discussion:
1. Is the article really needed?
2. Can the person(s) afford it?
3. Will the item purchased fill the purpose for which it is intended or needed?
4. Are there wiser ways to fill the need?

Summarize by emphasizing the need for all persons to be wise consumers.

13. WHO OWNS IT? (Grades 2-6)
VALUE: RESPECTING PROPERTY

A. Purpose: To help pupils respect the property rights of others.

B. Materials: Chalkboard.

C. Procedure: Discuss the following three types of property ownership:

1. Private property: e.g. Things that belong to you which others should not use without your permission.

2. Corporate property: e.g. Things that belong jointly to you and a small group of others such as other members of your family which any member of the group can use.

3. Public property: e.g. Things that belong to the general public which are available on an equal basis to all.

Draw a chart on the chalkboard with three columns with the headings shown below:

Private Property	Corporate Property	Public Property

Ask pupils to name various objects and the column in which you should write them.

Summarize the activity by pointing out that just as we want people to respect our property, so we should respect the property of others and public property.

14. PRIVATE PROPERTY--KEEP OUT (Grades 3-8)
VALUE: RIGHT TO PRIVACY

A. Purpose: To encourage pupils to honor the right of privacy of others.

B. Materials: Pupil's desk, locker, notebook, purse, teacher's desk and other personal possessions.

C. Procedure: Place a small sign on one of your desk drawers marking it, "Private Property-Keep Out".

Explain to the class that this drawer is for your use only and that you expect the pupils to honor your right to privacy by not opening it.

Point out that they, as well as all other persons in the room, have a similar right. We honor this right by not looking in one another's notebook, digging through one another's desks or lockers, or by reading one another's papers.

Apply the principle publicly often enough to set the example pupils can follow in this regard by making statements such as the following:

John, since your desk is your private property, I would like you to look through it for the paper that is missing.

Mary, please look through your notebook for me to find the outline we need.

15. NEEDS OR WANTS? (Grades 4-8)
VALUE: CONTENTMENT

A. Purpose: To help pupils realize that many things they want are not real needs.

B. Materials: A wide range of appealing advertisements of some items that are necessities for life and some items that are clearly luxuries. Small circles of cardboard.

C. Procedure: Make small circles of cardboard about 1 inch in diameter so they can be easily held in a child's hand without being seen by others. Make half of one color such as green and place a large "N" for need on them. Use a different color such as red or blue for the other half and print an "L" for luxury on them. Give one "N" card and one "L" card to each pupil.

Tell the class that you will show them pictures of items advertised for sale. If they consider the item to be a need, ask them to hold up the "N" card; if they think it is a luxury and not a real need, they should hold up the "L" card. All pupils should hold up their cards at the same time for counting. They should hold up the cards in such a way that only the teacher can see how the child is voting.

As each picture is shown, the teacher should record the voting count on the chalkboard in a chart like that shown below:

Item	Number of votes for "need"	Number of votes for "luxury"

After several pictures have been shown to the class, hold a discussion about needs and wants.

Summarize by pointing out that we will become very discontented if we want many things we do not need.

16. RETURNING A FEW PENNIES (Grades 3-6) VALUE: HONESTY

A. Purpose: To encourage pupils to make a serious effort to return any item that they find to its rightful owner.

B. Materials: Story of Abraham Lincoln walking several miles to return a few pennies to a customer because he had given him the wrong change.

C. Procedure: At a time when a pupil finds something of value but is unable to locate the rightful owner, tell the story of the time when Abraham Lincoln who was working as a store clerk, mistakenly gave the wrong change to a customer so that three cents more was due the person. Relate also how "Honest Abe" as he came to be called, walked several miles to return the extra few cents to the rightful owner. This example of real effort to return a few pennies is a good example of the effort we should expend to locate the rightful owner of any item we may find.

Solicit from your class a variety of ways that could be followed to find the owner of an item that was found. Carry these out as a class. If the owner is still not found, decide as a class what should be done and to whom the item now belongs.

17. HANDLE IT GENTLY   (Grades K-4)
VALUE: GENTLENESS

A. Purpose: To help pupils realize that handling some objects requires much gentleness to avoid damaging them.

B. Materials: Several very fragile but beautiful items such as a painted eggshell, a flower, a dandelion seed ball, etc., and a few strong, solid items such as an iron bolt and a wooden ruler.

C. Procedure: Show the articles to the class and list them on the chalkboard in the left column of a chart like that shown below. In the second column write the qualities of the item and in the third put down the words or ideas that the pupils suggest about how each item should be handled to keep from harming it.

Item	Qualities of the item	How item should be handled
Dandelion seed ball	Fluffy, comes apart easily	Don't jar it Don't blow on it Don't move it too fast

Next pass the items around the class and have pupils note differences in the care needed as they receive and pass along each item.

After the items have all been passed around the

class, look at them together. Use the following questions as discussion starters:
1. Were any of the fragile items damaged?
2. What does it mean when we say we must handle something gently?
3. When is gentleness important?
4. What kinds of things do we do each day that require gentleness?

D. Variation: When pupils bring "show and tell" or hobby display items that are especially fragile or easily broken, have a lesson on how to handle such items with gentleness.

18. LEARNING TO FISH (Grades 5-8)
VALUE: SELF-SUPPORT

A. Purpose: To stimulate in pupils the desire to be self-supporting, productive members of society.

B. Materials: Bulletin board space. Tape recorders.

C. Procedure: Mount this old Chinese proverb on the bulletin board:

"IF YOU GIVE A MAN A FISH,
   YOU FEED HIM FOR A DAY.
IF YOU GIVE A MAN A FISHHOOK,
   YOU FEED HIM FOR A LIFETIME."

Use the following questions to begin a discussion on the benefits of working for the things one receives:
1. How do you feel if you do something well and get paid for doing it?
2. Do you get more satisfaction out of earning the money you spend or out of simply receiving the

money as an "allowance" from your parents?

3. Do you help a person more if you give him a gift to supply his needs or if you teach him a skill so he can earn money for himself?

Use these questions and others that are related which the class formulates as the basis for taped interviews.

Divide the class into teams and provide each team with a tape recorder. Ask the team members to "interview" other students as well as teachers and parents to discover what their answers to the questions might be.

After all members have had an opportunity to serve as "interviewers", ask a committee of the class to listen to the taped responses and select a number to play back to the total class. They should also present a summary of the attitudes the responses reflect.

Conclude the lesson with a summary discussion. Attempt to draw out conclusions that highlight positive attitudes toward working for one's own self-support and the satisfaction a person receives when he/she is able to do so.

SECTION SEVEN

VALUES RELATED TO EDUCATION

Value development is continuous. As students live and grow and spend much time with their studies during school years, their values related to education are constantly being shaped. The activities in this section will enhance such value development while students are in the process of getting their education.

1. HOMEWORK FIRST (Grades 5-8)
VALUE: SELF-DISCIPLINE

A. Purpose: To help pupils build the habit of self-discipline so that they place completion of their responsibilities before play on their list of personal priorities.

B. Materials: A supply of 3 x 5 inch cards.

C. Procedure: After making a homework assignment, recognize with your class that many things may tend to distract us from completing it on time. Each person has things that are special distractions for him/her. For some, television may be a prime distraction; for others, it may be a sport, reading an interesting but irrelevant book, playing with a friend, etc.

Distribute the 3 x 5 inch cards to the pupils. Ask them to write the title: IMPROVING MY SELF-DISCIPLINE as a heading across the top. Next ask them to put down the following three sub-titles:

IMPROVING MY SELF-DISCIPLINE

I. My strongest distractions are

II. My plan to overcome them is

III. How well my plan worked

After having each pupil write down whatever his/her chief distraction is, ask the pupils to formulate a plan that will help them overcome the problem. Remind them that to succeed one must not only make a plan but one must also implement it. Ask the pupils to evaluate their success and complete the third section of the card.

D. Variation: Whenever pupils have a special problem in achieving self-discipline, have them use one of the cards to make a plan and work to overcome the distractions.

2. LIBRARY BOOK RETURNS (Grades 3-8)
VALUE: PUNCTUALITY

A. Purpose: To develop a sense of the importance of punctuality through a study of the library book return habits of the students in your school.

B. Materials: Access to the book return records of the patrons of your school library.

C. Procedure: Discuss the need for punctuality in the return of library books. Use the following questions as discussion starters:

    1. Why do libraries loan books only for a limited period of time such as two weeks?

    2. What penalties does your library have if pupils do not return books on time?

    3. When one student isn't punctual in returning a book he/she has borrowed, how does this inconvenience other library users?

Appoint a committee to make a study of the punctuality patterns of the pupils who borrow books from your school library. Gather information from the librarian through a one month study of the number of books loaned out, the number returned on time, the number turned in late, and the number lost or that will likely never be returned.

Have the committee make a report to the class of their findings. Ask them to include the advantages of being punctual both for the borrower and the rest of the school community.

D. Variation: Work with the librarian of a nearby public library to make a similar study. Compare the punctuality pattern of the patrons of the public library with that of the students using the school library. Relate the value "punctuality" to the value "courtesy" and "consideration for others" as it relates to the use of the community library.

3. IS YOUR DESK WELL-ORGANIZED? (Grades 3-7)
VALUE: ORDERLINESS

A. Purpose: To encourage pupils to maintain orderly desks by showing them that messiness keeps us from doing our best work.

B. Materials: Regular pupil desks for storage of books, pencils, paper, etc. Pencils, rulers and paper for making "blueprints". Stopwatch.

C. Procedure: Discuss with your pupils the way that desks can be organized. You may wish to have them experiment with ways in which their books and materials can be arranged. Take into account the size of the various books they have been issued as well as the order and frequency in which they are used. When a good way has been agreed upon, draw a "blueprint" on the chalkboard. Have the pupils make a similar diagram on a sheet of paper. If the pupils have desks that have tops that lift up, have pupils mount the "blueprint" inside the lid with scotch tape.

Have timed tests, using a stopwatch, so that pupils discover for themselves how much more quickly they can locate the books they need if their desks are well-organized than if they are not.

D. Variation: If the pupils have desks with lids that do not lift up, the blueprint can be kept as a large wall poster for all to see, or the small individual blueprints can be taped to the corner of the desks.

4. WHY STUDY THIS? (Grades 4-8)
VALUE: USEFULNESS OF STUDY

A. Purpose: To establish the usefulness of studying English by contesting the arguments pupils bring against its value.

B. Materials: A person to play the role of adversary, such as a college student home on a visit, a successful business man, or the director of a local employment agency.

C. Procedure: At a time when class members question the value of developing good speech habits or learning the rules of grammar and English usage, invite a resource person to your class.

Explain that some of your class members see no reason why they should learn to write and speak correctly.

Have the class present their arguments for not learning good English usage, then have the resource person present his/her point of view arguing the points from the perspective that the person holds.

D. Variation: When a pupil raises the question, "What good will learning this do?", find out what type of work he/she hopes to do some day or what type of profession that student would like to enter. Locate a business firm or professional person to whom the student could write a letter asking if the matter in question is related to success in that field of work.

5. WHEN OTHERS MAKE MISTAKES (Grades 3-8)
VALUE: KINDNESS

A. Purpose: To have pupils show empathy for one another rather than ridicule when someone makes a mistake.

B. Materials: Illustrative instances when your class members have made mistakes. Poster paper, felt pen.

C. Procedure: Write this old proverb on a sheet of poster paper.

"KINDNESS IS TO DO AND SAY,
THE KINDEST THING IN THE KINDEST WAY."

Display it in some prominent place in the classroom.

Explain to the class that there are many ways by which we can show kindness to one another but that it is most important to show kindness by not ridiculing, laughing at or making fun of the mistakes of others.

To teach the kind way to react when someone makes a mistake as opposed to unkind ways to do so, choose a number of situations appropriate to your classroom and school such as the following:

    1. The class is holding a discussion and someone makes an irrelevant or incorrect comment or expresses a point of view that differs from the point of view of most class members.

    2. Several pupils in a math class are asked to work their problems on the chalkboard. All pupils work the problem correctly except one who gets the process confused.

    3. A spelldown is being held in your class and a child "let's down his team" by spelling a word incorrectly.

4. The pupils "choose sides" for a playground ball game. Everyone is chosen except the last child who is known to be a poor player.

Divide the class into groups and have each group select a situation from the list or another or their own and role play the situation twice; once showing an unkind way and once showing a kind way to handle it so that no one is ridiculed.

D. Variation: When a situation arises in which a child is treated unkindly, discuss alternative ways by which others could more properly and kindly have reacted and role play the better responses. Have pupils evaluate how they would feel if they were the person who made the mistake in each case.

6. CHEATING ON A TEST (Grades 4-8)
VALUE: HONESTY

A. Purpose: To help pupils understand that cheating on a test is both dishonest and harmful to ourselves.

B. Materials: A test.

C. Procedure: Before you ask your class to take a test, talk about the need for honesty on the part of everyone taking it. Ask why honesty in taking tests is important. Make the following points:

1. Cheating is dishonest because it is a form of stealing. Stealing an answer is similar in many ways to stealing anything else that one does not own. The Christian religion as well as other religions teaches that stealing is morally wrong. Stealing is declared to be wrong by the laws of civil government as well and is punishable in various ways.

2. Cheating is harmful to the person taking the test because the score received does not then give an

honest assessment of one's ability and achievement. This will lead to more serious problems in the future.

3. Cheating is an affront to the teacher and other class members.

Discuss with your class ways in which the temptation to cheat can be removed such as in the following:

How can we be seated so no one will be tempted to copy the answers from another person's paper?

Where can we put our books, notes and other study materials so we will not be tempted to look at them?

How can we prepare for the test so as to avoid the need to cheat?

How can we use the test results so that honest answers will be most helpful to students' learning?

Summarize the discussion to help pupils sense the importance of honesty.

7. IT'S RAINING (Grades 1-4)
VALUE: BOOK CARE

A. Purpose: To help pupils realize that books need special care to protect them in rainy weather.

B. Materials: A book that has been left out in the rain and has been badly damaged. Plastic book-sized bags with name labels.

C. Procedure: Choose a rainy day for this learning activity. Show the class the damaged book and ask the pupils if they know what could have happened to ruin it.

After they have suggested or you have told them that it had been left out in the rain by someone who did not have enough concern about its welfare, have children examine the book to note that it is now both unpleasant in appearance and useless.

Next arrange a spot in your classroom where pupils can pick up a plastic bag to put their books in if they need to take them home for a homework assignment on a rainy day. Have them make out a label so the bag with the book can be identified in case it becomes lost.

Encourage pupils to bring a few empty plastic bags from home to build up the supply on hand for use when necessary on rainy days.

D. Variation: Use a note to the parents or an announcement at a Parent-Teacher Meeting to inform the parents of your students about the system you have for having the children protect their books on all rainy days. Solicit their cooperation in encouraging their children to care for their books especially on rainy days.

8. SIFTING FACTS FROM OPINIONS (Grades 4-8)
VALUE: FOUNDING OPINIONS ON FACTS

A. Purpose: To help students differentiate between facts and opinions and to found their opinions on facts.

B. Materials: Pictures of Indians with feathered headdresses living in tepees. Pictures of Indians on and off reservations today. Bulletin board space. 3 x 5 inch cards.

C. Procedure: Mount the caption, WHAT I KNOW ABOUT INDIANS, at the top of a bulletin board space. Distribute several 3 x 5 inch cards to each student and ask them to write something that they have heard or read about Indians on each card. After a sizeable number of such cards have been completed, collect them.

Next divide the bulletin board into three parts with yarn as shown below:

WHAT I KNOW ABOUT INDIANS		
FACTS	NOT SURE IF THIS IS FACT OR OPINION	OPINIONS

Appoint a committee to read the cards and mount them in one of the three sections.

Have another committee recheck the placements made by the first committee. Then have pupils do research about the comments on the cards in the middle part to determine if they should be placed in the "Facts" or "Opinions" section.

When all cards have been removed from the center sections, hold a summarizing discussion using the following questions as discussion starters:

1. What is the difference between a fact and an opinion?

2. What did you learn about your opinions about Indians?

Conclude by emphasizing the need to form opinions carefully.

9. FACT OR FICTION (Grades 4-7)
VALUE: ACCURACY OF HISTORY

A. Purpose: To help students distinguish between what is true and what is myth or fiction in our understanding about what life was like at the time of the exploration and settlement of the American West.

B. Materials: History books and other library research materials about life in the American West. 3 x 5 inch cards.

C. Procedure: Have the class imagine they are a group of settlers just starting out on their journey westward on the Oregon or Santa Fe Trail. Ask them to gather around an imaginary campfire and hold a "story telling time".

Encourage everyone to participate by "spinning a yarn" that is, telling something they read or heard about traveling conditions or about the area of the West where they hoped to go.

As the stories are told, keep notes about the ideas or supposed facts expressed. Write each such fact or idea on a separate 3 x 5 inch card.

Next give one card with its "supposed" fact or idea to each student.

Have students do research to confirm or disprove what is written on the card received. When all have had opportunity to do so, hold a second campfire story time to see if the stories have changed.

Summarize the activity by emphasizing the difference between imaginative stories and accuracy in history.

10. **FOR OR AGAINST (Grades 4-8)**
    VALUE: EXPRESSING CONVICTIONS

A. Purpose: To encourage pupils to express their convictions and to state the rea ons for them.

B. Materials: Samples of "Instapol" questions from the newspaper, 3 x 5 inch cards, bulletin board space.

C. Procedure: Introduce the lesson by mounting the caption on the bulletin board:

QUESTION FOR THE DAY

FOR   AGAINST

Note with your class that many national newspapers and even separate national polling companies attempt to assess the opinions of people every day about political questions, the popularity of national leaders, or even the type of TV program they prefer.

Explain that a new question will be put up on the bulletin board each day. Pupils should think about the question as individuals and write their responses in the following form on a 3 x 5 inch card:

    I am _____ (for or against)
_____ (the topic of the day)
because _____
_____.

After completing a card, the students should mount them on the appropriate side of the bulletin board.

Questions may vary from current political issues on the international level to classroom rules or school problems.

Encourage pupils to express their convictions and the reasons for them clearly and to respect the convictions of others.

D. Variation: Divide the class into groups with some pupils for an issue and some against it in each small group. Have them attempt to resolve the issue in a way to which all can agree.

11. LEARNING CONTRACTS (Grades K-8)
VALUE: SELF-RESPONSIBILITY

A. Purpose: To give pupils an opportunity to share in setting learning goals and responsibility for achieving them.

B. Materials: A variety of learning contracts.

C. Procedure: Identify the reluctant learners in your classroom and arrange a conference with each to draw up a learning contract with them in some chosen area of the curriculum. A good contract should have the following characteristics:

1. The task agreed upon should be meaningful and relevant to the life and interests of the student.

2. The task should be achievable to allow for a high degree of success so they need to be geared to the student's academic abilities and needs.

3. The task to be done should be clearly defined so evaluation can be readily and promptly completed.

4. The time for completion should be included in the contract.

5. Limit the length of the work included in any one contract to small tasks or short assignments at first and lengthen these as the child is able to assume more responsibility.

6. A space for the signatures of both the student and the teacher should be provided.

As students work on their contracts, emphasize the importance of the student's sense of self-responsibility in keeping the contract that was drawn up and signed.

12. MATH SKILLS APPLIED (Grades 4-8)
VALUE: GOOD CITIZENSHIP

A. Purpose: To help pupils realize the many ways they must apply math skills to be good citizens.

B. Materials: Regular math assignments, daily newspapers, chalkboard.

C. Procedure: As you begin a new unit in your math program, try to find every possible way in which the skill to be learned is related to the problems faced by adults in the "real world".

Display a copy of the daily newspaper each day and choose the examples used in presenting the math lesson from the advertisements and news stories.

Discuss the many ways that good citizenship depends on the ability to use math accurately and honestly.

13. SUCCESS RECORD (Grades K-6)
VALUE: SELF-CONFIDENCE

A. Purpose: To enhance pupils' self-confidence by having them record or to record for them, one success experience per day.

B. Materials: A small notebook, either of the commercial type or pupil-made.

C. Procedure: Provide a small notebook for each pupil or have pupils make one by stapling a number of pages about 3 x 5 inches in size together.

Distribute the booklets to the pupils near the end of each day. Ask them to think of one thing that happened at school that day that they felt went very well for them. This could be a lesson, an answer that they gave or a game with a friend. Ask them to write the day's date and draw a picture of or write a few sentences about the successful experience. Collect the booklets each day when the pupils have finished. For pupils who think that nothing went well, you may have to make suggestions of good things that you noticed that the child did.

Continue the experience for a few weeks. Then ask pupils to go over the things they had written or drawn. Help them identify the kinds of things they have been able to do successfully over a period of time and thus encourage their self-confidence.

14. EXERCISING SELF-DISCIPLINE (Grades 2-8)
VALUE: SELF-DISCIPLINE

A. Purpose: To strengthen the students' ability to exercise self-discipline.

B. Materials: A supply of 3 x 5 inch cards.

C. Procedure: Introduce the idea of self-discipline to the class by asking how many pupils were faced with the task of doing something they didn't really like to do but made themselves do it anyway because it needed to be done.

Follow this with a discussion of the many times when self-discipline is needed. Use the following instances as examples.

1. Keeping your mind on your school work and getting the work finished even though you would rather watch what others are doing.

2. Turning off the TV and doing your homework.

3. Practicing your music lesson before going outdoors to play.

4. Choosing foods that are best for you rather than simply those that taste the best.

5. Getting out of bed when you are first called

or coming in promptly from recess when the bells ring.

Have the class add a number of other instances from their own experience.

Next provide the class with 3 x 5 inch cards. At the end of each day have pupils write an example of something they did that day which shows they exercised self-discipline. Have them put a smiling face in an upper corner of the card as a self-reward.

Collect the cards each day for one week. Send the cards home to the child's parents at the end of the week with a special note expressing appreciation for the child's efforts to develop self-discipline.

D. Variation: Follow the same "end-of-the-day" evaluation on a total class rather than an individual basis. Have pupils suggest things that went well and also list ideas for things that could be improved the next day to make the classroom tone more pleasant for everyone. Note how it will require self-discipline on the part of all to achieve the goal.

15. TATTLE TALE (Grades 1-5)
VALUE: PROBLEM-SOLVING

A. Purpose: To help pupils distinguish between situations when a problem should be reported to adults immediately and when it should be resolved between pupils themselves.

B. Materials: Bulletin board space, 3 x 5 inch cards.

C. Procedure: Mount the following caption on your bulletin board:

TATTLE TALES --- YES or NO???

Report to Adults as soon as possible	Uncertain	Try to resolve first, report only if unsuccessful

Introduce this learning activity at a time when pupils seem to be too eager to tattle on one another.

Call the attention of your class to the bulletin board. Then distribute a 3 x 5 inch card to each pupil. Ask the pupils to write one playground or other school situation on the card. Ask them to mount their finished card on the bulletin board in one of the three columns.

Pupils in the lower grades may state the situation and you can record it on a card and place it on the bulletin board in the column of the pupil's choice.

After the cards have been placed on the bulletin board, hold a discussion to emphasize the difference between situations involving danger and possible harm to someone which should be reported to a responsible adult immediately and other situations where there are petty differences of opinion which pupils should do their best to resolve themselves.

Encourage pupils, however to ask for your advice as to possible ways to solve the problem to guide the choices they make.

D. Variation: When someone "tattles" about some small issue, instead of simply making a ruling as teacher, arrange a time when the parties involved can discuss the issue and, if possible, resolve the problem independently.

16. WELCOMING COMMITTEE (Grades K-8)
VALUE: MAKING NEW STUDENTS FEEL WELCOME

A. Purpose: To insure that new students who join your class are made to feel welcome and are helped to adjust to their new school environment.

B. Materials: New students and a welcoming committee.

C. Procedure: Introduce this learning activity after school has been in session in the fall for two or three weeks so that the class has generally come accustomed to their new classroom.

Schedule a discussion time when you can raise the following questions with your class:

1. How many pupils have transferred from one school to another? What different schools have they attended?

2. What kinds of things do transferred pupils worry about or are difficult for them to adjust to when they arrive in a new school?

3. How could we make a new pupil feel welcome if someone should arrive tomorrow?

Follow this discussion with the appointment of a "Welcoming Committee" in order that your class may be ready if and when a new student arrives.

D. Variation: Work with your school Parent-Teacher Association to welcome the parents of the children to the school community as well.

17. DESK NAME CARD (Grades 2-8)
VALUE: POSITIVE SELF-IMAGE

A. Purpose: To provide opportunity for pupils to strengthen the self-image of one another.

B. Materials: Poster board, scotch tape, felt pen.

C. Procedure: Cut a piece of poster board approximately 14 inches long and 9 inches wide for each pupil. Fold the long way in 3 inch sections and tape into a triangle shaped tube.

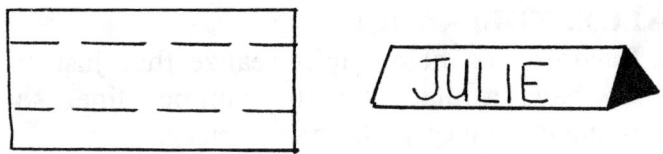

Print the child's name on all three sides. Have the pupils place these desk name cards on their desk so others, including yourself, will be able to learn their names quickly at the opening of the school term.

Then have pupils write positive (no negative) things about one another on desk cards of their classmates. Using pens with various colored ink will make the desk cards even more attractive in appearance. Pupils should initial the nice comments they write on someone else's desk name card. As teacher, you should find time to write something nice on each pupil's desk name card as well.

Summarize the activity after a period of time by discussing the following questions:

    1. How did you feel when you wrote something nice on someone else's name card?

    2. How did you feel when someone wrote something nice on your card?

    3. Were there some things you wish someone had written on your card that were not written there? What can you do so others will think of you in this way.

After pupils are well-acquainted with the names

of one another, have the pupils take their desk name cards home as mementos of your class.

18. NUMBER LINE (Grades 3-7)
VALUE: TOLERANCE

A. Purpose: To help pupils realize that just as all numbers have a place on the number line, so all persons have a place in human society.

B. Materials: A number line that shows both the positive and negative numbers.

C. Procedure: Mount the number line across the front of your classroom in the manner shown below:

$$\longleftarrow \mid \mid \mid \mid \mid \mid \mid \mid \mid \mid \mid \mid \mid \mid \mid \mid \mid \mid \mid \longrightarrow$$
$$-9\ -8\ -7\ -6\ -5\ -4\ -3\ -2\ -1\ \ 0\ \ 1\ \ 2\ \ 3\ \ 4\ \ 5\ \ 6\ \ 7\ \ 8\ \ 9$$

Make normal use of the number line in teaching the number system in your mathematics classes. On some appropriate occasion, compare the millions of people living on the earth with the numbers on the number line. Use the following questions to begin the discussion:

1. Does every number have its own place on the number line?

2. Is the number line complete when a number is missing?

3. Do all human beings have a place in human society?

4. Are all people different in the same way that the numbers are different?

5. Why should we be tolerant of the differences of other people? How can we show this tolerance?

6. Could we have a number line if all the

numbers were the same? What would our society be like if all people were the same?

Summarize the discussion by pointing out how different each member of the class is from every other member and yet how each contributes to the whole group. When one person is absent from school, it is like a number missing from the number line.

19. USE IT TOGETHER (Grades 2-6)
VALUE: SHARING

A. Purpose: To provide opportunity for pupils to practice sharing through having them use materials together.

B. Materials: One-half the number of books or materials normally used for a selected class activity.

C. Procedure: When the teacher distributes books for pupil use, research materials, art projects materials, etc., a copy of each book or article of learning materials is normally provided for each pupil so the pupils can work independently.

For this learning experience, the teacher should deliberately plan to provide only one half the usual number of books or supplies such as crayons, etc., normally required thus forcing pupils to share.

Before the distribution and use of materials, talk about the need to share with their partner and the need to do equitably and congenially.

Summarize the activity by discussing how we can improve our skills in sharing.

SECTION EIGHT

VALUES RELATED TO CULTURE

In the year 390 the greatest library of the ancient world, the library of Alexandria was destroyed and its contents burned. When the Huns overran Greece, much of the art of Athens was ruined. Later the Gauls sacked Rome. History teaches us that things that are good and beautiful have not always been valued. The activities in this section provide opportunities for students to develop positive values about culture.

1. WHAT IF WE HAD NO MUSIC? (Grades 4-8)
VALUE: MUSIC APPRECIATION

A. Purpose: To enable pupils to sense the many ways that music enriches their lives.

B. Materials: Bulletin board space, scissors, writing materials, old magazines from which pictures could be cut.

C. Procedure: Mount the caption, "WHAT IF WE HAD NO MUSIC?" on your bulletin board with four sub-headings as shown below:

WHAT IF WE HAD NO MUSIC?

Music is made by	Music is carried by	Music helps us by	If we had no music life would be

Introduce the consideration of music appreciation by having your class list some of the ways by which music is made. Write the suggestions of the pupils on the chalkboard. They may suggest, the songs of birds, the chimes of clocks or bells, the playing of various instruments, the human voice, etc.

Next discuss the topic listed at the top of the second division of your bulletin board, the ways in which music is conveyed to us. Again write the suggestions of the pupils on the chalkboard. They may list record players, tapes, radio, television, direct performances, etc. After discussing these first two columns, allow the class a day or two to find pictures of the ideas suggested and mount them in the first two divisions of the bulletin board.

When a substantial number of pictures have been mounted in the first two columns, find an appropriate time at which to discuss the two right hand columns. Discuss the headings of these two columns by having pupils present their ideas of ways in which music helps us and what life would be like if there were no music in the world.

After an introductory discussion to stimulate their ideas, distribute writing paper and ask them to write a brief paragraph or theme to mount in either the third or fourth column.

Allow individual pupils or small groups freedom to go to the bulletin board area and read the papers mounted there at an appropriate time in their daily class schedule.

D. Variation: Provide a prize of a record or tape for the best theme.

2. THE FIRST THANKSGIVING (Grades K-6)
VALUE: THANKSGIVING

A. Purpose: To strengthen the pupils' sense of thanksgiving for blessings enjoyed today through comparison with the life of the Pilgrims at the time of the first American Thanksgiving celebration.

B. Materials: Library resources dealing with the life and times of the Pilgrims. Bulletin board space.

C. Procedure: About the first week of November display the following caption on your room's bulletin board:

THANKSGIVING

For the Pilgrims   For Us

Select library resource materials appropriate to the grade level of your class about life at the time of the Pilgrims and about the celebration of the first Thanksgiving. Use the following questions as discussion starters as you consider the topic of Thanksgiving with your class:

1. Why is Thanksgiving Day celebrated in the fall of the year?

2. What kinds of things were the Pilgrims thankful for at the time of the first Thanksgiving Day celebration in America?

3. What was their way of life like? How did it differ from our way of life?

4. What kinds of things do we have to be thankful for?

Use the discussion to introduce the idea of building a class Thanksgiving season bulletin board. Ask the pupils to look through magazines at home and cut out pictures of things that the Pilgrims were thankful for at the time they lived and things for which we may be thankful today. Have each of the pupils mount these on the appropriate side of the bulletin board as they bring them to school during the weeks before Thanksgiving Day in November.

At an appropriate time just before the Thanksgiving Day holiday, conclude the activity by asking various pupils to identify the pictures they brought and to give the reasons why they thought it appropriate. Include a general discussion of the topic of thanksgiving and its place in our lives.

D. Variation: Instead of having pupils look for a and cut out pictures, have them draw appropriate pictures.

3. HISTORICAL AMNESIA (Grades 6-8)
VALUE: APPRECIATION OF ONE'S PAST

A. Purpose: To help pupils develop a sense of appreciation for their own history.

B. Materials: Some occasion when the study of history is introduced or the value of its study is brought into question.

C. Procedure: On an occasion when you are expected to introduce a unit in the study of history or if a pupil asks why it is necessary to "study this stuff about all those old guys", introduce the idea of amnesia. A person who is suffering from amnesia does not know who he is, where he came from, who his family or relatives are, etc.

Role play several situations in which pupils "lose their memory". Use some situations such as the following:

    1. A person who is on a busy street corner waiting for a bus who suddenly doesn't know who he is or where he was going.

    2. A child in school who suddenly can no longer speak English or remember the alphabet.

    3. A nurse at work in a hospital nursing station who suddenly forgets everything she has learned.

    4. A factory worker on an automobile assembly line who suddenly loses his memory of the use of his tools and of his job responsibilities.

After the role playing situations, discuss how much we depend on yesterday for what we do today. Have pupils make a list of the things that would be different or even impossible if they would suddenly be cut off from their past.

Summarize the activity by discussing how not knowing anything about one's own history is like suffering from amnesia. Include emphasis on how knowing about the past enriches one's present life.

D. Variation: Add the idea of studying one's family "roots" to learn more about who one is and what he is like.

4. WHERE DID WE GET OUR CUSTOMS?
(Grades 5-8)
VALUE: CULTURE ASSIMILATION

A. Purpose: To help pupils realize that many of the customs we follow today come to us from peoples of other cultures and times.

B. Materials: Chart paper, poster paper and felt pen. Library resource materials on customs.

C. Procedure: Discuss various customs followed by pupils in your class and by other members of your community. List these customs on a large piece of chart paper with your felt pen. Include items such as the following:

1. Special kinds of foods or ways in which food is prepared.
2. Special kinds of clothing worn for selected occasions.
3. Special ways of observing seasonal holidays.
4. Special kinds of art or crafts.
5. Special observances related to religious festivities or worship services.

Next distribute the poster paper. Have the pupils select one of the customs listed as the title or theme of the poster. Library materials should be used for research in connection with the custom selected. Pupils should use the information they find as the basis for completing their posters. Parents and other adults in the community may also be used as resources for information about the sources of the customs.

After the posters have been completed, have the pupils share the information they discovered by presenting and interpreting their posters to the class. Conclude the activity by summarizing the many sources of the customs we observe today and note with your class the many ways these customs enrich and add meaning to our lives.

D. Variation: Invite members of various ethnic and culturally different groups to come to speak to your class about the customs they observe and the meaning of them.

5. USING SCIENTIFIC KNOWLEDGE (Grades 5-8) VALUE: RESPONSIBILITY

A. Purpose: To help pupils realize that people living today have both far more scientific knowledge and responsibility to use this knowledge in the right way than did people living many centuries ago.

B. Materials: A list of man's comparatively recent advances in scientific study. Chalkboard space.

C. Procedure: Put the following column headings up on the chalkboard.

Recent inventions and scientific discoveries	Potential for good of mankind	Potential for harm to mankind

Begin the lesson by telling how mankind has benefited from such recent discoveries as atomic power. If a nuclear power plant is located in your state or region and supplies electrical energy for

—180—

your area, refer to this as one good result of this comparatively recent scientific discovery. Next discuss the potential danger of the discovery of the atom including atomic warfare and harmful radiation. Note with the class that this great discovery has both potential for good and for evil to mankind. Enter "atomic energy" as the first item on your chalkboard chart and complete the first lines in columns two and three as well.

Next ask the pupils to make a similar chart on a sheet of paper at their desks and to copy in the first item from the chalkboard as a model.

Suggest the automobile as a second item. Note both good and bad things about it. Then ask the pupils to add to their lists using whatever resources are available including talking to their family members at home.

Establish a given time such as one day later or one week later when the pupils will report their lists to the class.

Conclude the learning activity by discussing the importance of the responsibility for using scientific knowledge for good rather than for the harm of mankind.

6. WHO PRODUCED IT? (Grades 3-6)
VALUE: APPRECIATION OF EFFORTS OF OTHERS

A. Purpose: To help pupils appreciate that the things they use and enjoy are produced by many people in many different occupations and places.

B. Materials: A pair of shoes, a box of cereal, a bat and ball, a few other items that the pupils in your class particularly enjoy. Chalkboard.

C. Procedure: Write the question, "Who produces the many things we can use and enjoy today?" on the chalkboard. Call the attention of the class to the question and accept and write two or three answers given on the board in a form like that shown below:

Objects used or enjoyed	By whom or where they were produced

Next divide the class into groups of three to five pupils each and give each group an object such as a pair of shoes, a box of cereal, etc. Have the groups make a study of all the materials used in making the object and the persons involved in doing so. For example, the shoes involve leather which in turn requires ranchers, cattlemen, truckers, butchers, tanners, etc. The shoes also involve nails which require miners, smelters, manufacturers, etc. Shoes require laces which in turn, require another whole group of suppliers.

Each of the groups could make charts showing all the people and processes involved in producing the object studied. Have the groups report the results of their study to the class.

Hold a summary discussion focusing on building appreciation for the many things we use and enjoy each day.

D. Variation: Have a person from a local shoe store come to your class as a guest speaker to explain all of the processes involved in providing a pair of shoes.

7. FAMILY HEIRLOOMS (Grades 1-5)
VALUE: APPRECIATION OF FAMILY HEIRLOOMS

A. Purpose: To impress pupils with the sentimental value of articles that children receive from their parents and grandparents.

B. Materials: A family heirloom that you treasure such as an old picture, handkerchief, etc.

C. Procedure: Show the class the family heirloom that you have. Explain to them to whom the heirloom had previously belonged and how you came to have it.

Explain to the class that once such old materials become lost, broken or destroyed, they can never be replaced.

Use the following questions as discussion starters:

1. Does a thing have to have a real market value in order to be valued by someone?
2. Why do we often value things given to us by our parents and grandparents?
3. How can we best preserve things that are old and precious?

8. HEROES IN HISTORY (Grades 4-7)
VALUE: HEROISM

A. Purpose: To help pupils realize that America's heroes come from many races and national backgrounds.

B. Materials: History textbooks and other library references.

C. Procedure: Introduce the idea of national heroes in connection with a study of the history of our nation.

Begin by having pupils name heroes with which

they are familiar. Next have them do research to expand the list to include those who come from many races and national backgrounds.

Have each pupil select one hero of particular interest to him/her. Help the students locate library materials for use in doing research and writing reports about the person chosen.

Summarize the activity by pointing out that the heroes of our country in the past as well as leaders who serve our country today come from many different races and national backgrounds.

9. SONG ANALYSIS (Grades 4-7)
VALUE: APPRECIATING THE CONTENT OF SONG

A. Purpose: To help pupils relate the words of a song with the era in which it was written.

B. Materials: The words of several songs related to various eras of history, for example "Yankee Doodle", "Oh Susanna", etc.

C. Procedure: Hold a song fest when your class has opportunity to sing a wide variety of songs written in various eras of our country's history.

Note with your class that music is often the expression of the feelings and concerns of people living at the time that the song was written.

Have different groups of pupils each choose a song for study in an effort to relate the words of the song to lives of people who were living at the time of its writing. Allow each group to present the information they found and have them lead the class in the singing of that song.

D. Variation: Designate a special day as "Yankee Doodle" day, "O Susannah" day, etc. On such a special day pupils would be encouraged to wear costumes of the people represented in the song or living at the time that song was written. Also on that day, have special reports about the life and times the song was written and about the life of the person who wrote the words and the music. Have the class learn the song by singing it several times throughout the day.

10. LIBRARY BOOK CHARACTER DAY
(Grades 3-6)
VALUE: A GOOD CHARACTER

A. Purpose: To help pupils evaluate the character of others by role playing them.

B. Materials: A variety of library books. Poster paper.

C. Procedure: Introduce the idea of a "Character Day" to your class and set the date for about two weeks later. Explain that each student is to select and read a library book and choose a favorite character from the story.

On "Character Day" each student is to dress like the story book character. Provide poster paper to allow pupils to make hats appropriate for the character chosen if they wish to do so.

During the course of the day, plan a time when each student will have the opportunity to role play a small part of the book before the class. Encourage the students to not only portray the character and tell something about the book each has read, but also assess the character as to his/her good and bad qualities.

Encourage pupils to choose "good characters" from literature of the past rather than bad ones as models for their lives today.

D. Variation: When introducing this learning activity wear the costume of a book character and read or tell about a small portion of the book chosen in order that pupils may have a clearer idea of what you expect of them.

11. TIME CAPSULE (Grades 5-8)
VALUE: CHOOSING A MEMENTO

A. Purpose: To encourage pupils to think seriously about what is really important to them.

B. Materials: Resource materials about Egyptian pyramids, about burial customs of Egyptian kings and relics of King Tut. Location of some local buildings with cornerstones.

C. Procedure: Present the information and show the pictures you have of the Egyptian pyramids and the relics of King Tut.

Point out that we learn about civilizations of the past by digging up and studying the relics that archaeologists have found.

Note the present day custom of placing a metal box with information about present day life behind the cornerstone of a new building and sealing it with concrete.

Investigate whether or not your high school has a custom of having students place their names in a metal box under a special square in the sidewalk marked with the date of their graduation. If so, have a high school teacher come to your class to tell why and how this is done.

Next imagine that your class would have the opportunity to fill a "time capsule" which would be sealed and buried to hopefully be discovered by someone a thousand or more years in the future.

Each pupil would be allowed to place one thing in the capsule. What would it be? What is really important to them so that they would want to and be willing to share it with someone living in the future?

After the pupils have chosen, ask them to explain their choice to the class telling of what value they hope their memento will be to those who discover it.

12. LANGUAGE DIFFERENCES (Grades 3-8)
VALUE: APPRECIATION OF LANGUAGE AS A MEANS OF COMMUNICATION

A. Purpose: To help pupils appreciate language as a means of communication by noting the many different languages spoken.

B. Materials: Several dual language dictionaries such as English/Spanish, English/German, English/Russian, etc., tapes or books of a variety of languages, map of the world.

C. Procedure: Introduce the idea of language as a means of communciation within a given culture. Note how communication flows easily because all persons within the culture speak and understand the same language. Look at the world map with your class and identify areas of the world where the following major languages are spoken: English, German, Russian, Japanese, Portugese, French, Bengali, Hindustan, Italian, Spanish and Chinese.

Next identify as many other areas where less common languages are spoken in the world such as Polish, Dutch, Hebrew, Swedish, Korean, Arabic,

Hungarian, etc. Try to list as many as possible with your class.

Use the bi-language dictionaries to learn the meaning of several words in more than one language. Make a chart similar to the following showing the same list of words in several languages:

ENGLISH	SPANISH	GERMAN	FRENCH	RUSSIAN

Choose languages as column headings that are of interest to your class and about which you have information.

Note the problems of persons who are immigrants and come to a country where they cannot understand, read, speak or write the language used by the new country.

Help pupils develop an appreciation for the importance of language as a means of communication as you summarize the learning activity.

D. Variation: Have persons from the community who speak more than one language or foreign language instructors from a local high school or college come to your class to introduce the advantages of knowing more than one language.

13. RENAISSANCE ART (Grades 6-8)
VALUE: ART APPRECIATION

A. Purpose: To help pupils appreciate the art of the Renaissance period by classifying it by themes.

B. Materials: A collection of pictures of painting and sculpture of the Renaissance period. Bulletin board space.

C. Procedure: Mount the caption, "THEMES OF RENAISSANCE ART" at the top of a large bulletin board space. Divide the space below into sections with headings such as the following:

THEMES OF RENAISSANCE ART

Nature is beautiful	Persons are beautiful	God is to be praised

Appoint a committee of pupils to study the pictures and select one to be mounted under each theme. Have a committee member explain to the class something about the painting or sculpture and the life of the artist.

Allow students to come up to the bulletin board and study the pictures carefully during any free time they have during the day.

Appoint other committees for each day over a one or two week period depending on the number of pictures available.

Hold a summarizing discussion on the art work of the Renaissance period and the themes evident in it.

D. Variation: Follow this study of art during the Renaissance period with a similar activity using modern art. Have the class develop the theme and column headings.

14. HANDICAPS OF GREAT PEOPLE (Grades 5-8)
VALUE: OVERCOMING HANDICAPS

A. Purpose: To help pupils realize that everyone has certain strengths and weaknesses and that some people have overcome severe handicaps to rise to greatness.

B. Materials: Library research materials. 3 x 5 inch cards.

C. Procedure: Begin the learning activity by mounting the caption, "DID A HANDICAP HOLD THEM BACK?" on the bulletin board. Then hold a class discussion about the differences evident in the people in your community. For example, an excellent banker might be a poor truck driver, an excellent musician might be a poor athlete, and excellent teacher might be a poor businessman and an excellent telephone repairman might be a poor doctor. Emphasize the need to use the talents and body size, the mental abilities, etc., that are yours personally in such a way to achieve success and contribute to the welfare of society.

Next point out that many persons who have contributed a great deal to our culture have been handicapped in one way or another. Have each pupil choose some person from the present or the past who has made or is making a real contribution to culture and society and do research on that person to see if there was some particular handicap that the person overcame to achieve success.

Have pupils report their findings to the class and write a brief summary on a 3 x 5 inch card to mount on the bulletin board.

D. Variation: If there is a person in your community who is handicapped and who is successful in his/her life's work, invite the person to speak to your class.

15. WITHOUT PREJUDICE (Grades 2-8)
   VALUE: ACCEPTANCE OF OTHERS

A. Purpose: To reduce pupil prejudice against persons with other ethnic backgrounds.

B. Materials: Social studies curriculum materials. Chart paper.

C. Procedure: As you begin studying various countries and the cultures of the world in social studies, make a chart on a sheet of chart or poster paper approximately 2 x 3 feet in size. In the left column list a number of topics that are common to all cultures such as the following:

	Country	Country	Country	Country
Clothing Styles				
Favorite Foods				
Types of Housing				
Arts and Crafts				
Games and Customs				

Encourage pupils to suggest additional topics for study or select those emphasized in your social studies materials and add these to the left column.

As you study the various cultures and countries, write the name of each at the top of the columns at the top of the chart. Enter items in the chart as each new country or culture is studied so that you will have many items listed by the end of the school term.

Summarize each time a new column is added so that you build a cummulative appreciation for the similarities and differences but especially the contribution of all the countries of the world to our culture today. Emphasize the idea of cultural differences without becoming judgmental.

D. Variation: Whenever possible use resource persons from your community by having persons from various ethnic backgrounds or who have travelled or lived in other lands come to speak to your class. Ask them to comment particularly on the topics you have listed on your chart.

16. CHRISTMAS CUSTOMS (Grades K-8)
VALUE: APPRECIATION OF DIFFERENCES IN CUSTOMS

A. Purpose: To help pupils appreciate and understand the Christmas customs of various cultures.

B. Materials: Library resource materials about Christmas customs, resource persons from various ethnic groups.

C. Procedure: Make a study with your class of the ways in which Christmas is celebrated in various parts of the world.

Have pupils form groups of from 3 to 5 members each. After each group has selected a particular country or culture to study, have them do research on the Christmas customs of that country and report their findings to the class. Encourage pupils to use pictures and music in making their reports.

D. Variation: If possible, have resource persons representing various ethnic groups within your community come to speak to your class about the Christmas customs they observe.

17. STARTING A NEW COLONY (Grades 5-8)
VALUE: A BALANCE OF SKILLS

A. Purpose: To help pupils appreciate the wide variety of skills needed to make a well-rounded community.

B. Materials: Chalkboard, a list of skills, trades, businesses and professions.

C. Procedure: Have your class name as many skills, trades, businesses and professions as they can. Include those that are well-known such as dentist, truckdriver, farmer, teacher, etc., as well as some the children are less likely to think of such as pharmacist, draftsman, tailor, etc. Write these on the chalkboard as they are suggested by the class and as you supplement their suggestions.

When the list is sizeable and reasonably complete, divide the class into groups of three.

Tell them to imagine that a new colony is to be settled on a newly discovered planet. The space ship will hold the three members of the committee plus only ten others and their families. Each committee must look at the different types of skills represented in the list on the chalkboard and select the ten they feel are most essential to build a new community successfully.

When each group has its list prepared, compare the results and have each group explain their choices.

Summarize the activity by discussing the kinds of

career choices the students need to make and the way the careers they choose affect the lives of the community in which they will live.

18. VISITING THE SYMPHONY (Grades 2-8)
VALUE: COOPERATION

A. Purpose: To strengthen the student's sense of the importance of cooperation.

B. Materials: A visit to a symphony orchestra program, a record of symphony music or a movie of a symphony playing. A tuba, base violin, and several other instruments; school instrumental music teacher and selected students.

C. Procedure: Have the class attend a symphony orchestra program or listen to some symphony music on a record. Note with your class how the beauty of the music is produced by many persons playing the many different types of instruments in harmony.

Invite the instrumental music teacher of your school system to bring a group of selected students with their various instruments to your class to demonstrate the musical capabilities of each. Note how each instrument has something special to contribute to the beauty of music when played in harmony with other instruments.

Next discuss the importance of cooperation in producing symphonic music. Use the following questions as discussion starters:

1. What would happen to the beauty of the music if one instrument tried to dominate all the others?

2. What would happen to the beauty of the music if some of the instruments would not do their part?

3. What would happen to the fullness of the

music if each instrument played only by itself?

4. What would happen if none of the players paid any attention to the conductor?

Conclude the discussion by considering with your pupils the many ways in which your class, your city or your family is like a symphony orchestra because of the need to cooperate. Have the class list as many ways as possible in which cooperation is important. Compare results when persons cooperate and when they do not.

D. Variation: Have members of your class who take instrumental music lessons organize a small music group. Ask them to play one number in harmony for the class. Next have them play the same number with all kinds of obvious discord. Discuss the difference in the results emphasizing the need for cooperation in production of good music. Apply this to various life situations.

SECTION NINE

VALUES RELATED TO ENVIRONMENT

Thoughtless use of our forests, depletion of our mineral resources, contamination of our streams and lakes, littering of our cities and the pollution of the air all reflect a distorted sense of values. The activities in this section will encourage students to build values that prompt wise concern for the environment.

1. TURN OFF THAT UNUSED LIGHT (Grades 5-8)
VALUE: SAVING ENERGY

A. Purpose: To encourage pupils to save electrical energy whenever possible.

B. Materials: Information about the cost of electricity, the sizes of light bulbs and the wattage of various electrically operated household appliances. Several light bulbs of various sizes. An electric toaster.

C. Procedure: Introduce the topic by teaching how electricity is measured. Show the light bulbs to the class and have them read the watt sizes shown on them. Have pupils make a chart similar to the following. Ask the pupils to make a list of the light bulbs used in their homes and then record for one week, the time they were in use.

ROOM	LIGHT BULB SIZES	NUMBER OF HOURS USED							TOTAL ELECTRICITY USED
		S	M	T	W	T	F	S	

Next show the pupils the toaster and note with them the place on it that shows how many watts of electricity it used while in use. Tell how pupils can read the wattage of other household appliances on the appliances themselves or in the instruction manuals that accompany them when they are purchased. Next have pupils make a list of the electrical appliances that they have in their homes and the electric current usage of each on a chart similar to the one shown below:

Type of appliance	Electric current wattage	Hours used S M T W T F S	Total electricity used

Have pupils total the amount of electricity used for one week and multiply it by the cost per kilowatt hour.

Discuss how electricity is produced and how it makes life more pleasant for us. Next consider ways in which you could save electricity and avoid the waste of this natural resource. Have the class make a real effort to save electricity whenever possible and record the amount used again for a second week. Compare the totals to see how much energy was saved in just one week through everyone's special effort to avoid waste.

2. AVOID ACCIDENTS (Grades K-3)
VALUE: SAFETY

A. Purpose: To help pupils recognize things in their environment that are unsafe and potential health hazards.

B. Materials: Samples of familiar household items that are dangerous to health. Include those commonly found in the homes of children in your class. Newspaper articles and pictures that report various accidental injuries in your community.

C. Procedure: Begin the lesson by showing and reading the newspaper articles that tell about recent accidents in your community. Discuss ways in which such accidents could have been avoided.

Next present the items you brought with you to show to the class. Use the following questions for discussion starters:

1. Why are the items unsafe?
2. How can potentially harmful items be stored safely?
3. How could matches, plastic bags or old refrigerators be unsafe?
4. How can items that are normally safe when used correctly become unsafe when misused?

Conclude the discussion by pointing out the need for and value of safety.

D. Variation: Keep a list of the pupils who are absent from your school during a period of time such as one month or one semester. Try to classify the reasons for the absences according to the reasons why the pupil was unable to attend school such as illness, accidental injury, etc. Have your class make a special study of the absences due to accident and try to determine if there is some way such accidents could be prevented in the future.

3. WASH OUT (Grades 3-7)
VALUE: CONSERVATION

A. Purpose: To help pupils realize that bare soil can be washed away and lost but soil that is covered with some type of vegetation will not erode as quickly.

B. Materials: A variety of pictures of land that has been eroded by water. Two trays each about 4-6 feet long and about 1 foot wide. Soil, sod, water and pans.

C. **Procedure:** Show the class your pictures of land that has been eroded by water. Introduce the terms erosion, flash flood, sediment, wash-out.

Discuss the problem of soil erosion using the following questions as discussion starters:

1. According to some geologists it may take hundreds of years for one inch of topsoil to be formed. Why do you think this is such a slow process?
2. If topsoil is washed away into streams, how does it affect the quality of the water and the environment for fish?
3. How does erosion affect the productivity of land?

Next set up a demonstration of how erosion works. Mount the trays with one end about three or four inches higher than the other so they have a slight slope. Fill one tray with soil and the other with a strip of sod dug up from the edge of a garden or other available place. The sod strip could also be obtained from a lawn and garden store.

Next have the pupils measure out two similar amounts of water, about one to three gallons, depending on the length of your trays. Have them pour an equal amount of water at the top end of both trays at the same time as shown below:

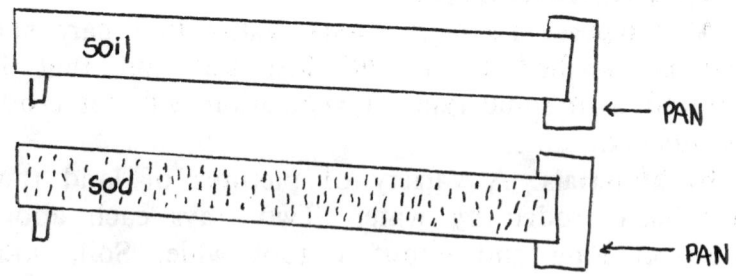

Be sure that the pans are properly placed at the bottom end of the trays.

Note the following with your class:

1. How long did it take for the water to go from the top to the bottom of the tray? (Record the time.)

2. What difference is there in the amount of water in the two pans? Why this difference?

3. What difference is there in the amount of sediment in the bottom of the pans? Why this difference?

Conclude the learning activity by discussing ways in which erosion can be prevented and soil saved.

4. **DON'T BE A LITTERBUG (Grades 5-8)**
   VALUE: COMMUNITY CLEANLINESS

   A. Purpose: To help pupils build the habit of placing trash and other waste materials in proper containers.

   B. Materials: Clearly marked waste containers in the classroom, halls, restrooms and on the school property. Official badges.

   C. Procedure: Discuss the problem of littering in America--
   --on the streets of a city
   --in parks and other public places
   --along the country's highways
   --in your school

Include possible reasons why people litter.
   --inconvenient to place trash in containers
   --don't care whether environment is clean
   --don't care enough about others

Initiate a "Don't Be a Litterbug" campaign. Have pupils make official-looking badges to wear.

These could be obtained commercially if a badge printing shop is available in your community or they could readily be made on strong cardboard that would last for a week's campaign. The badges would be of any shape desired by the child and attached with a safety pin or mounted on a pocket insert as follows:

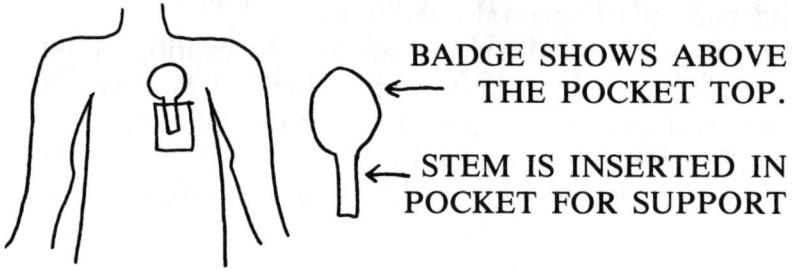

BADGE SHOWS ABOVE THE POCKET TOP.

STEM IS INSERTED IN POCKET FOR SUPPORT

The badge slogans should be the original ideas of the class. Several of the suggestions of the pupils could be written on the board. The pupils could then vote on the slogan all would wear or a variety could be used.

An official "anti-littering pledge" could also be made up and recited by the class each day of the campaign week.

During the week the pupils should not only not litter themselves, but should clean up trash wherever it is found. An organized playground clean-up might be part of the week's activities.

D. Variation: The use of plastic trash bags for your clean-up officials would be helpful to show how much trash each pupil or team of pupils had collected during the week. Arrange for a reward activity at the end of the campaign.

5. WRITE YOUR OWN PICTURE CAPTION
(Grades 5-8)
VALUE: WHOLESOME ENVIRONMENT

A. Purpose: To help pupils express their ideas about various environmental conditions.

B. Materials: A wide variety of pictures equal to the number of pupils in your class reflecting good and bad environmental conditions.

C. Procedure: Make a study of the captions used by newspapers to capture the chief idea about a news picture. Note how the caption tells the key idea portrayed in the picture.

Number the pictures from 1 to the number of pupils in your class and give one picture to each pupil. Provide a sheet of paper for each pupil and have them list numbers in the left margin up to the total number of pictures distributed.

Ask the students to study the picture they have and write a brief caption for it on the line number which is the same as the picture number.

Have pupils pass the pictures around the room in a prescribed system and write a caption for each so that when the pictures have made a complete circuit, every pupil will have a numbered page with a caption for each picture.

Mount the pictures on the bulletin board along with the lists of captions. Have pupils vote on the best caption and award the picture to the winner in each case.

Have the winner of each picture tell what characteristic of the environment whether good or bad was most striking in the picture.

6. ALWAYS IN THEIR OWN ORBIT (Grades 3-8)
VALUE: DEPENDABILITY

A. Purpose: To give students a sense of security through increasing their awareness of the dependability of the solar system.

B. Materials: A model of and information about the solar system.

C. Procedure: Draw a model of the solar system on the chalkboard similar to the one shown below:

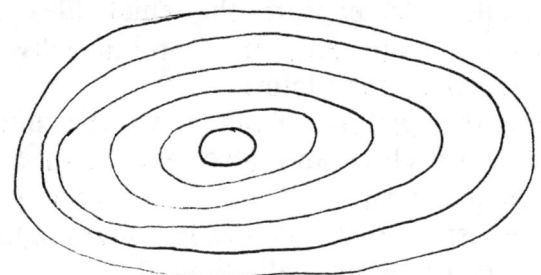

Discuss the meaning of the following terms:
  Rotation: Earth turning on its axis causing day and night.
  Revolution: movement of a planet in its pathway around the sun.
  Orbit: pathway a planet follows in its revolution around the sun.

Next consider the regularity of the movements of the planets within the solar system. Note how astronomers who study the movements of heavenly bodies can predict the precise time of an eclipse or the coming into vision of a comet many years in advance of when these events occur.

Move the discussion to a thoughtful speculation about how important it is to the lives of plants, animals and human beings that we can depend on the sun rising and setting regularly and what would happen if it would not.

Conclude the exercise by having pupils draw a picture with two parts as follows:

THE SOLAR SYSTEM IS DEPENDABLE	IF THE SOLAR SYSTEM WAS NOT DEPENDABLE

Ask pupils to display their pictures and explain the drawings to the class.

7. EXTINCT (Grades 5-8)
VALUE: PRESERVATION OF SPECIES

A. Purpose: To make students aware of which species of birds and animals already are and which are in danger of becoming extinct.

B. Materials: Library reference materials about birds and animals.

C. Procedure: When an article appears in your newspaper that is related to a species of birds or animals that is nearing extinction, use that occasion to introduce this learning activity.

Bring the article to school; read it to and discuss it with your class. For example, if the article is about a hunter being fined for shooting an eagle, begin the study with questions like the following:

1. Why do we have laws that protect eagles rather than starlings?

2. Why should we try to protect the few eagles that are still living?

Appoint a special committee to prepare a list of birds and animals that have already become extinct or are in danger of doing so. Ask them to report the list to the class. Next have the rest of the class form groups with each group selecting one bird or animal from the list for a more detailed study and report.

8. OUR ORDERLY SEASONS (Grades K-3)
   VALUE: AWARENESS OF THE ORDER IN NATURE

A. Purpose: To make pupils more aware of the order evident in nature by observing the changing seasons.

B. Materials: Art supplies for making a mural.

C. Procedure: At a time of the year when seasons are changing such as the beginning of winter or the coming of spring, have the children make a large classroom mural. Use the caption and divisions show below:

OUR ORDERLY SEASONS			
Spring	Summer	Fall or Autumn	Winter

Discuss with your class the kinds of backgrounds the different parts of the mural should have. Next discuss the kinds of special activities that occur during each of the seasons and the activities of people, birds and animals as well as the changes in trees and plants.

Divide the class into groups to cut out pictures to be pasted or drawn on the mural.

As the pupils work on the project and decide where various pictures should be drawn or pasted, emphasize the orderliness and dependability of the seasons.

D. Variation: Give each child a sheet of drawing paper and have him divide it into four quarters. In each quarter have him draw an activity related to one of the seasons.

9. WHO NEEDS WATER? (Grades 2-8)
VALUE: APPRECIATION OF WATER

A. Purpose: To help pupils appreciate the importance of water.

B. Materials: Bulletin board space, writing materials and library research materials about water.

C. Procedure: Select a very rainy day for this exercise when pupils are somewhat disgruntled because the rain limits their outdoor play.

Begin the activity by asking the class if they wish the rain would stop. If they could make it stop, when would they make it rain again?

Move the discussion to the importance of water as you attempt to make them less disgruntled with the rainy day. Put the following caption at the top of a bulletin board space:

WATER IS IMPORTANT FOR _____
BECAUSE _____.

Ask the class for a few examples. They will likely respond with items such as "Water is important for parents because they need it to wash clothes". or "Water is important to firefighters because they need it to put out fires".

Next announce a contest to see who can think of the most uses for water. Have each child make a list numbering each entry. Allow them to work on it immediately to get it started and throughout the day during any spare time they may have. Allow them to include ideas from their general knowledge and library research materials or use their other textbooks for ideas. Near the end of the day, have the pupils tell how many uses of water they were able to think of and mount their lists on the bulletin board so pupils can read the lists of one another.

Give the pupil who has the longest list the privilege of getting a drink of water as the prize.

Conclude the exercise by pointing out that although the rain may be unpleasant in some ways it is very necessary in many others.

10. WASTING WATER (Grades 4-8)
VALUE: CONSERVATION OF WATER

A. Purpose: To show pupils how much water is wasted through a leaky faucet and what could be done to stop this waste.

B. Materials: A leaky faucet, a pail or other water measuring container, a few faucets and washers.

C. Procedure: At a time when you are studying the conservation of our natural resources, bring up one of the ways in which water is frequently wasted, namely, through neglecting to maintain faucets properly.

Locate a faucet that drips steadily even when attempts are made to shut it off. If none can be located, make one drip that would be similar to what might be found in another place.

Have the pupils guess how much water is wasted because of the dripping. Record the guesses.

Next have a committee collect the water over a 24 hour period in an appropriate container and then measure the amount with a pint or quart container. Multiply the amount of water wasted in one 24 hour period by the number of days in a year to determine the total amount wasted by one dripping faucet each year. Have pupils imagine that each house represented by the families in the school has one dripping faucet. Then have pupils attempt to determine the cost of this wasted water.

Next have pupils take the sample faucets apart to see how they work. Also have them practice replacing the washers in them.

D. Variation: Invite a plumber to your class to demonstrate how dripping faucets can be repaired.

11. YOU CAN'T LIVE WITHOUT IT (Grades 5-8)
VALUE: APPRECIATION FOR CLEAN AIR

A. Purpose: To strengthen pupils' awareness of the importance of clean air.

B. Materials: Library research materials and art materials for poster construction.

C. Procedure: Begin by having pupils count the number of times they breathe each minute while they are seated at their desks. Next have pupils "run in place" besides their desks for one minute and make a second count to note how much the breathing rate increases when the body exercises strenuously.

Have a committee make a study of the breathing rate of various animals such as elephants, horses, dogs and mice. Compare the breathing rate of animals with their size.

Next raise the issue of how long human beings, animals and plants could live without air to breathe.

Since air is so important to life, discuss with your class if we are doing enough to protect its purity.

Have pupils design and make a poster emphasizing the need for pure air.

D. Variation: Have a committee of students make a study of their community to look for possible sources of air pollution or check with major industries to discover what precautions they have taken to prevent air pollution.

12. A PARK OR A PARKING LOT (Grades 5-8)
VALUE: PRESERVING NATURAL RESOURCES

A. Purpose: To help pupils realize that preservation of natural areas is difficult.

B. Materials: A desk map of your local area for each pupil or a larger one for wall display.

C. Procedure: Distribute a desk map of your local area to each student or if these are not available mount one larger map on a bulletin board wall display.

Develop a system of color coding for parks and parking lots (such as green for parks and black for parking lots).

With your class make a study of your city or extended community in order to enter all parks and parking lots on the maps.

After the study has been completed, compare the area used for each purpose.

Conclude the learning activity by role playing a situation in which your city has a serious downtown parking problem. Discuss the pro's and con's of solving the problem by converting a downtown park or lawn into a parking lot.

13. MINERAL DEPOSITS (Grades 4-8)
VALUE: APPRECIATION FOR MINERAL DEPOSITS

A. Purpose: To enable students to better appreciate the wide variety of mineral deposits in the earth.

B. Materials: Library research materials, bulletin board space, construction paper fragments of various shapes and sizes, felt pens.

C. Procedure: Mount the caption, "MINERAL RICHES OF THE EARTH" on the bulletin board. Then provide felt pens and a large number of fragments of construction paper nearby where pupils can select one of their choice. Have them write the name of one mineral on each piece of paper and pin it on the bulletin board in a random pattern.

After pupils have put up the names of familiar minerals, have them do added research to locate the names of as many additional minerals as possible.

When the students have listed as many different minerals as they could find, discuss the wide range of minerals being mined and the importance of each to business and industry.

D. Variation: Include a world map in the bulletin board display and use yarn to connect the name of the mineral to one important location where it is mined.

14. COLLECT AND RECYCLE (Grades 4-8)
VALUE: RECYCLING RESOURCES

A. Purpose: To provide an opportunity for pupils

to participate in a recycling project.

B. Materials: Information about local markets for recycled paper, aluminum cans, glass, iron, etc.

C. Procedure: Investigate the possibility of recycling and marketing some type of waste material that is available in your community. After insuring yourself of a market for the material collected, appoint a committee of your class to organize a collection campaign. Ask them to give thought to the following aspects of the project:

1. How will collecting this item help the environment?

2. What process will the industry where the material is marketed use to recycle the material collected?

3. How will the funds received for the collected materials be used?

After all plans have been carefully made, advertise the project to obtain community support and carry out the collection for recycling campaign.

15. PREVENT FOREST FIRES (Grades 4-7)
VALUE: FIRE PREVENTION

A. Purpose: To make pupils aware of the high cost of forest fires and ways they could be prevented.

B. Materials: Library research materials about forest fires. Poster making materials. Pictures of forest fires.

C. Procedure: Show your pictures of forest fires to the class and discuss the topic of forest fires with them. Use the following questions for discussion starters:

1. What kinds of forest fires can we do very little

to prevent?

2. What kinds of forest fires can be prevented?

3. How do forest fires affect the lives of animals and birds in the fire area?

4. What precautions against fire should be taken by persons who go hiking and camping in wooded areas?

Move the discussion to a poster-making exercise. Encourage pupils to formulate a catchy but meaningful slogan as their poster title. The slogans should be related to the topic of forest fire prevention.

D. Variation: Work with a local camping equipment retail store to sponsor a forest fire prevention poster contest at your school.

16. WHEN THE ELECTRICITY IS OFF
(Grades 2-5)

VALUE: APPRECIATION OF ELECTRICAL POWER

A. Purpose: To make pupils more aware of how much electricity helps us.

B. Materials: Chalkboard, writing and drawing materials.

C. Procedure: Use this learning activity just after the electrical service has been interrupted in your community.

Have pupils tell how many things didn't work at their houses while the electricity was off. Write these on the chalkboard as the pupils name them. Add any others that the pupils had overlooked. You should attempt to have as long a list of electrical appliances, etc., as possible.

Next discuss how these many things that use electricity help to make our lives more comfortable and interesting.

Move to an individual pupil activity and allow pupils to choose one of the following:

1. Draw a divided picture with one half showing how our homes would be without electricity and the other half with electricity available.

2. Write a paper telling how people lived before electrical power was available.

Conclude the learning activity by emphasizing the advantages of electrical power and the many ways it helps to make our lives more pleasant.

D. Variation: Have pupils do research on how the electrical power that is used in your community is produced.

17. KEEP OFF THE GRASS--DON'T PICK THE FLOWERS (Grades K-5)
VALUE: OBEYING RULES

A. Purpose: To encourage students to obey signs about lawns and flowers.

B. Materials: Two signs--DON'T PICK THE FLOWERS and KEEP OFF THE GRASS (or other similar signs familiar to your pupils).

C. Procedure: Show the signs to the class and ask if the pupils have ever seen signs similar to them. As pupils respond affirmatively, write the information on a chart similar to the one shown:

WORDING OF SIGN	LOCATION OF SIGN	REASON FOR SIGN BEING PLACED THERE

Include not only the wording and location of the sign but get pupils to suggest the reason why they think the sign was placed as it was.

After several have been listed, have the pupils suggest "What If" answers. For example, "What if everyone disobeyed the sign and each picked a flower?"

Summarize the activity by emphasizing the need to obey the signs placed for the public good.

D. Variation: Have a committee from your class interview the person who cares for the school grounds or local parks to discover what the general reaction of the public is to their signs.

18. GROUND HOG DAY (Grades 5-8)
VALUE: RESPECTING THE SCIENCE OF WEATHER STUDY

A. Purpose: To build a sense of respect for the science of weather study and an appreciation for its importance.

B. Materials: Information from the local weather bureau on the equipment and science of weather prediction. *Old Farmer's Almanac.* Information about Ground Hog's Day.

C. Procedure: On or about Ground Hog's Day, which is always on February 2nd, explain to the class that for many years people believed they could use the groundhog's habits to predict weather. If the groundhog came out of his burrow on Ground Hog's Day and saw his shadow (this required a sunny day) he would be frightened and return to his burrow and the weather would remain cold and wintery. It would then be about six weeks before he would come out again. This would mean that spring would be late.

Refer also to the *Old Farmer's Almanac* for many old sayings about the weather used by early pioneers in forecasting weather conditions. Have pupils ask their parents and other older relatives if they know any old proverbs or sayings that relate to weather prediction.

Discuss why accurate weather prediction is of vital importance to farmers, fishermen, pilots, etc.

Next have the class do research about modern systems of predicting weather. If possible take a field trip to a weather station.

Summarize the activity by reviewing with your class the many ways that the work of the weather bureau is helpful to you.

D. Variation: Discuss with your class the reasons why many people ridicule or blame the weatherman. Include situations such as the following:

    1. It rained when sunshine was predicted.

    2. A severe storm warning was issued and no storm arrived.

    3. A severe storm came and advance warning was given too late.

Summarize by building empathy for the weatherman by pointing out that he doesn't cause the weather but only tries to predict it as accurately as possible.

19. ARBOR DAY (Grades K-8)
VALUE: REFORESTATION — APPRECIATION OF TREES

A. Purpose: To help pupils appreciate the beauty of trees and realize that forests are a replaceable resource.

B. Materials: A class tree and space to plant it.

C. Procedure: Arrange with your school's administration or local park authorities for a spot where your class can plant a tree.

Make a study of the kinds of trees that grow well in your geographic area. Have the class select one variety and develop a plan with them so that all children can contribute something toward the purchase of a tree of that type from a local nursery.

Study also the best way to plant a tree to insure its growth.

Have the class participate in the process of planting and caring for "their" tree.

Identify the tree with a small sign as "planted in the year ____ by the ____ grade class of _____ school."

Encourage the pupils to continue their observation of the tree's growth in the future.

D. Variation: Visit a nursery or tree farm with your class and make a study of modern methods of forest replanting.

20. NOISE POLLUTION (Grades 5-8)
VALUE: NOISE CONTROL

A. Purpose: To help students realize that noise control laws have both a good and bad side.

B. Materials: An audiometer, information about the noise control laws that apply to your local area.

C. Procedure: Teach students to operate the audiometer by measuring various sounds in the classroom.

Review the noise control laws that govern your local area. Decide with your class where some of the noisiest places are in your community. Include such places as a street intersection, a road traveled by school buses, etc.

Poise a dilemma such as the following:

1. School buses are too noisy to drive through a residential area to pick up pupils.

2. A fuel delivery truck is too noisy to bring gasoline to a local station.

3. A snow plow or other type of road maintainance equipment is too noisy to be allowed to care for your street.

4. An airplane is too noisy to land or take off at your local airport.

Appoint a committee to make a number of audiometer readings in the community and report their findings to the class.

Note with your class that noise control has real benefits for people who might otherwise be subject to excessive noise pollution but such laws sometimes limit the kinds of mechanical or technological services that could be provided.

D. Variation: If a violation of local noise control laws is registered by the committee taking audiometer readings, discuss the best way to report this to the offenders.

21. WHEN A TREE BURNS (Grades K-4)
VALUE: FOREST FIRE PREVENTION

A. Purpose: To help pupils realize the many products made from trees and the costly damage of forest fires.

B. Materials: Bulletin board space. Yarn, old magazines and scissors.

C. Procedure: Begin this learning activity by mounting the caption and design shown on your bulletin board:

WHEN A TREE BURNS, WHAT GOES UP IN SMOKE?

Discuss with your class the many kinds of products used today that are made from trees. Have pupils find pictures of as many such products as possible, cut them out and mount them inside the yarn outline of a tree on the bulletin board.

Summarize the learning activity by noting with your class how many products are made from trees and what a great loss a forest fire causes.

INDEX

SECTION ONE: VALUES RELATED TO ONE'S PERSON
Chapter One: Values that are chiefly unseen or internal.

TITLE	K	1	2	3	4	5	6	7	8	PAGE
1. What a Long Time to Wait!	x	x	x	x	x					2
2. Scars					x	x	x	x		3
3. Solving Shyness				x	x	x	x			4
4. How Are They Different?	x	x	x	x	x					6
5. Dealing With Your Feelings						x	x	x	x	6
6. Are You A Puppet?					x	x	x	x		8
7. You Decide	x	x	x	x	x					9
8. All About Me	x	x	x	x						10
9. You Can Choose Only One						x	x	x	x	11
10. These Are A Few Of Our Favorite Things	x	x	x	x	x					12
11. Mirror, Mirror On The Wall	x	x								14
12. Passive Or Agressive							x	x	x	15
13. I Meant To Do My Work Today					x	x	x	x		16
14. I'm Glad I'm Not A Tree	x	x	x	x						17
15. The Sun Is Always Shining				x	x	x	x			18
16. Changing Faces				x	x	x	x			19
17. I Wish				x	x	x	x			20
18. Honesty Haiku				x	x	x	x			21
19. Examine The Consequences Or Results				x	x	x	x	x	x	22
20. Value Center				x	x	x	x			23
21. Do Clothes Make The Person?				x	x	x	x	x		25
22. How Much TV?			x	x	x	x	x			26
23. Personal Preferences	x	x	x	x	x	x	x	x	x	27
24. Accepting Praise Graciously				x	x	x	x	x	x	28
25. Fingerprints					x	x	x	x	x	30

SECTION ONE: VALUES RELATED TO ONE'S PERSON
Chapter Two: Values that are more external and are often expressed in words and actions.

TITLE	K	1	2	3	4	5	6	7	8	PAGE
1. Look At The Bright Side	x	x	x	x	x					33
2. Good Manners Morning				x	x	x	x			34

TITLE	K	1	2	3	4	5	6	7	8	PAGE
3. Let's Put Fruit On The Helpfulness Tree	x	x	x	x	x	x				35
4. What Is Leadership?				x	x	x	x			36
5. Help Wanted						x	x	x	x	37
6. Like Dominos		x	x	x	x	x	x	x	x	38
7. Serve As A Travel Consultant					x	x	x	x	x	39
8. Analyzing Inconsistencies						x	x	x	x	40
9. Planning Your Time						x	x	x	x	41
10. Courtesy Mobiles	x	x	x	x	x	x	x	x	x	43
11. Choosing A Pet	x	x	x	x	x	x				44
12. A Four Way Test				x	x	x	x	x	x	45
13. A Timely Topic	x	x	x	x	x	x	x	x	x	46
14. Who Do You Trust?					x	x	x	x	x	47
15. Lost And Found				x	x	x	x			48
16. Agreeable or Disagreeable					x	x	x	x	x	49
17. A Contest	x	x	x	x	x					50

SECTION TWO: VALUES RELATED TO THE FAMILY

TITLE	K	1	2	3	4	5	6	7	8	PAGE
1. My Family Is Where I Belong	x	x	x							53
2. What Parents Do For Us	x	x	x	x						53
3. Send A Card		x	x	x	x	x				54
4. Helping At Home	x	x	x	x	x					55
5. Where Have You Been?			x	x	x	x				57
6. Roots							x	x	x	58
7. Pleasantness In Unpleasantness				x	x	x	x	x	x	59
8. Housekeeping Corner	x	x	x							60
9. Task Choices					x	x	x	x	x	61
10. Table Talk Topics				x	x	x	x	x	x	62
11. Family Members Bill Of Rights						x	x	x	x	63
12. Caring For Family Property	x	x	x	x	x	x				64
13. Comic Strips Speak				x	x	x	x	x	x	65
14. Showing Love	x	x	x	x						66

TITLE	GRADE LEVEL	PAGE

TITLE   GRADE LEVEL
                 K 1 2 3 4 5 6 7 8

SECTION THREE: VALUES RELATED TO OUR HUMAN RELATIONSHIPS

	K	1	2	3	4	5	6	7	8	PAGE
1. The Blind Men And The Elephant					x	x	x	x	x	69
2. Winners Or Losers						x	x	x	x	70
3. Appreciation Time				x	x	x	x	x	x	70
4. Let's Play Ann Landers				x	x	x	x	x		72
5. Employer-Employee Relationships						x	x	x	x	73
6. I'm A Member					x	x	x	x	x	74
7. Cattlemen vs. Sheepherders						x	x	x	x	75
8. Little People			x	x	x	x				76
9. Because						x	x	x	x	77
10. Shadows	x	x	x	x	x					79
11. Potlatch					x	x	x	x	x	80
12. Consider Robin Hood						x	x	x	x	81
13. Helpers Club	x	x	x	x	x	x	x	x	x	82
14. War Or Peace					x	x	x	x	x	83
15. What's In A Name?				x	x	x	x	x	x	84
16. Choices Between Opposites					x	x	x	x	x	85
17. Don't Embarrass Others						x	x	x	x	86
18. Say Something Nice					x	x	x	x	x	87
19. Compliment Time	x	x	x	x						88
20. Persons Or Objects				x	x	x	x	x	x	89
21. No Man Is An Island						x	x	x	x	90
22. Things Done By And For Others				x	x	x	x	x	x	90
23. Shared Interest Groups				x	x	x	x	x	x	92
24. Making Introductions					x	x	x	x		93
25. Telephone Manners	x	x	x	x	x					93

SECTION FOUR: VALUES RELATED TO PERSONAL HEALTH

	K	1	2	3	4	5	6	7	8	PAGE
1. Should I Smoke?						x	x	x	x	96
2. Good Or Bad?					x	x	x	x	x	97
3. Cleanliness Chart	x	x	x	x	x					98
4. Growth Folder	x	x	x	x	x	x	x			99
5. Helen Keller's Lesson						x	x	x	x	100
6. Health Servant's Collage	x	x	x	x						100
7. Just Suppose					x	x	x	x	x	102
8. Is It Just Good Or Good For You?	x	x	x	x						103
9. Traits Or Habits			x	x	x	x				103
10. To Love Your Work						x	x	x	x	105

TITLE	K	1	2	3	4	5	6	7	8	PAGE
11. Working Through One's Hostile Feelings	x	x	x	x	x	x	x	x	x	106
12. How Do You Feel Today?				x	x	x	x	x		107
13. Rites Of Passage							x	x	x	108

SECTION FIVE: VALUES RELATED TO AUTHORITY AND GOVERNMENT

	K	1	2	3	4	5	6	7	8	PAGE
1. Would You Ride With Paul Revere?							x	x	x	112
2. Overtime Parking							x	x	x	113
3. Like The Pieces Of A Jigsaw Puzzle					x	x	x	x		114
4. Is Freedom Of Speech Really Free?				x	x	x	x	x		116
5. Righting Wrongs					x	x	x	x	x	116
6. Preamble Study							x	x	x	117
7. A Pledge Is A Promise	x	x	x	x						119
8. When Others Are Watching					x	x	x	x	x	120
9. Is It Fit To Eat?						x	x	x	x	121
10. Penalties For Drug Abuse							x	x	x	123
11. What Is A Law?			x	x	x	x				124
12. Make A Graph							x	x	x	125
13. On Trial							x	x	x	125
14. Not Like Lightning					x	x	x	x	x	126
15. Right, Wrong Or Maybe						x	x	x	x	127
16. Campaign Promises						x	x	x	x	128
17. Simulating Signing The Declaration Of Independence						x	x	x	x	129
18. Who Made The Rules?					x	x	x	x	x	130

SECTION SIX: VALUES RELATED TO PROPERTY

	K	1	2	3	4	5	6	7	8	PAGE
1. For Sale						x	x	x	x	133
2. If I Had A Million Dollars					x	x	x			134
3. Put It In The Bank		x	x	x	x	x				135
4. Analyzing Advertising						x	x	x	x	136

TITLE	K	1	2	3	4	5	6	7	8	PAGE
5. A Broken Window						x	x	x	x	137
6. Spray Paint							x	x	x	138
7. Finders Keepers					x	x	x	x		139
8. Choosing The Right Tool		x	x	x	x	x				140
9. Workaholics						x	x	x	x	141
10. When You Borrow Something		x	x	x	x	x	x	x		142
11. What Can I Do With Money?						x	x	x	x	144
12. Wise Consumers						x	x	x	x	145
13. Who Owns It?		x	x	x	x	x				146
14. Private Property--Keep Out					x	x	x	x	x	147
15. Needs Or Wants?						x	x	x	x	148
16. Returning A Few Pennies					x	x	x	x		149
17. Handle It Gently	x	x	x	x	x					150
18. Learning To Fish						x	x	x	x	151

SECTION SEVEN: VALUES RELATED TO EDUCATION

TITLE	K	1	2	3	4	5	6	7	8	PAGE
1. Homework First						x	x	x	x	154
2. Library Book Returns				x	x	x	x	x	x	155
3. Is Your Desk Well-Organized?				x	x	x	x	x		156
4. Why Study This?						x	x	x	x	157
5. When Others Make Mistakes				x	x	x	x	x	x	158
6. Cheating on a Test					x	x	x	x	x	159
7. It's Raining		x	x	x	x					160
8. Sifting Facts From Opinions						x	x	x	x	161
9. Fact or Fiction						x	x	x	x	162
10. For or Against						x	x	x	x	163
11. Learning Contracts	x	x	x	x	x	x	x	x	x	165
12. Math Skills Applied					x	x	x	x	x	166
13. Success Record	x	x	x	x	x	x	x			166
14. Exercising Self-Discipline			x	x	x	x	x	x	x	167
15. Tattle Tale		x	x	x	x	x				168
16. Welcoming Committee	x	x	x	x	x	x	x	x	x	170
17. Desk Name Card			x	x	x	x	x	x	x	170
18. Number Line				x	x	x	x	x		172
19. Use It Together			x	x	x	x				173

TITLE	GRADE LEVEL	PAGE
	K 1 2 3 4 5 6 7 8	

SECTION EIGHT: VALUES RELATED TO CULTURE

Title	K	1	2	3	4	5	6	7	8	Page
1. What If We Had No Music?					x	x	x	x	x	175
2. The First Thanksgiving	x	x	x	x	x	x	x			176
3. Historical Amnesia							x	x	x	178
4. Where Did We Get Our Customs?						x	x	x	x	179
5. Using Scientific Knowledge						x	x	x	x	180
6. Who Produced It?				x	x	x	x			181
7. Family Heirlooms	x	x	x	x	x					183
8. Heroes in History						x	x	x	x	183
9. Song Analysis						x	x	x	x	184
10. Library Book Character Day				x	x	x	x			185
11. Time Capsule						x	x	x	x	186
12. Language Differences				x	x	x	x	x	x	187
13. Renaissance Art							x	x	x	188
14. Handicaps of Great People						x	x	x	x	190
15. Without Prejudice			x	x	x	x	x	x		191
16. Christmas Customs	x	x	x	x	x	x	x	x	x	192
17. Starting a New Colony						x	x	x	x	193
18. Visiting the Symphony				x	x	x	x	x	x	194

SECTION NINE: VALUES RELATED TO GOVERNMENT

Title	K	1	2	3	4	5	6	7	8	Page
1. Turn Off That Unused Light						x	x	x	x	197
2. Avoid Accidents	x	x	x							198
3. Wash Out				x	x	x	x			199
4. Don't Be a Litterbug						x	x	x	x	201
5. Write Your Own Picture Caption						x	x	x	x	203
6. Always in Their Own Orbit				x	x	x	x	x	x	204
7. Extinct						x	x	x	x	205
8. Our Orderly Seasons	x	x	x	x						206
9. Who Needs Water?			x	x	x	x	x	x		207
10. Wasting Water						x	x	x	x	208
11. You Can't Live Without It						x	x	x	x	209
12. A Park or a Parking Lot						x	x	x	x	210
13. Mineral Deposits						x	x	x	x	211
14. Collect and Recycle						x	x	x	x	211
15. Prevent Forest Fires						x	x	x	x	212

TITLE	GRADE LEVEL									PAGE
	K	1	2	3	4	5	6	7	8	
16. When The Electricity Is Off				x	x	x	x			213
17. Keep Off The Grass--Don't Pick The Flowers	x	x	x	x	x	x				214
18. Ground Hog Day							x	x	x	x	215
19. Arbor Day	x	x	x	x	x	x	x	x	x	216
20. Noise Pollution							x	x	x	x	217
21. When A Tree Burns	x	x	x	x	x					218

DRAMA-PAK™

Each "Pak" contains a playbook for each main character and one for the director.

SCHOOL FOR ANGELS
A Fantasy - by Natalie Bovee Hutson
Six Main Characters

Less than one week until Christmas and chaos reigns in The Great Beyond! While Earth bombards the Heavenly Headmaster with urgent requests for "perfect" angels, it is discovered that the current "crop" is woefully lacking in "angel skills". Cherubs have been playing frisbee with the stars, conducting pillow fights with the clouds, and swinging from the Pearly Gates. The angel choir doesn't even know the words to "Silent Night"!
A delightful play for all ages and all seasons.
☐ 304-7..$9.95

THE GRUMBLE GROUP
A Comedy - by Natalie Bovee Hutson
Five Characters

The Grumble Group meets regularly (and grudgingly) at a city bus stop, where they find endless subjects about which to complain. On the surface these four individuals appear to be cantankerous old-timers, finding nothing right with the world. But as they reveal themselves to the audience, and through the help of an optimistic newcomer, it slowly becomes apparent that beneath the somewhat comic exteriors, lie sensitive people who have, for various reasons, become quite disenchanted with life.
A good choice for all ages.
☐ 301-2..$9.95

ME, BETH CONNORS
A Teenage Drama - by Natalie Bovee Hutson
Seven Characters

Meet Beth Connors, an average twelve-year-old, who through a series of flashbacks, takes the audience by the hand and leads them through a typical day in her life. It's a day filled with girlish giggling, a mysterious phone call, and the usual scraps with a pesky younger brother. But best of all, it is a day in which a routine visit to her grandmother in a nursing home, enables Beth to view life in a more adult manner.
☐ 303-9..$9.95

DRAMA-PAK™

Each "Pak" contains a playbook for each main characters and one for the director.

MR. TEDLEY'S TREEHOUSE
A Drama for the Young - by Natalie Bovee Hutson
Seven Characters

Mr. Tedley is a child's dream come true. He lives alone in a treehouse surviving on berries and nuts, offering friendship and vast knowledge to the younger set. But is he real? Ryan and Joey know that he is, but cannot convince others of the fact, and this troubles them.

In a simplistic way, the play deals with every child's need to fantasize and cling to dreams. Yet it also emphasizes that there comes a time when one must leave the fantasies behind and face the real world.

A charming play for young and old.

☐ 302-0..$9.95

THE READING OF THE WILL
A Farce - by Natalie Bovee Hutson
Seven Characters

Henry P. Jaybody may be deceased, but he is not absent from the reading of his will! Knowing that his greedy heirs would do their best to "out-mourn" each other, Henry had the foresight to plan a scene which would send the tribe in all directions, showing their true colors - and practically trampling one another in the process.

An action-filled play with characters who are fun to portray and even funnier to watch.

☐ 305-5..$9.95

THE WRONGFUL CLAIM
An Old-Fashioned Melodrama - by Natalie Bovee Hutson
Eight Characters

The lovely and innocent Melody Lark is but a servant in the home of wealthy Vanessa Vapors. Vanessa's avaricious daughter, Crystal, is envious of Melody's childlike charm and attentions of the gardener, Barnaby Barnhart. So when Crystal accidentally discovers that Melody is about to fall heir to a fortune, she plots her disinheritance. Unaware of his sister's scheme, an equally greedy Humphrey Vapors devises his own plot to discredit Melody.

An old-fashioned melodrama with lots of heroes and villains and a chance to hiss, boo, and applaud them all.

☐ 300-4..$9.95

DUPLICATOR BOOKS

Use our ideas in duplicator form to cut teacher preparation time and fulfill the needs for supplementary activities in the following areas of study:

LANGUAGE ARTS

☐ ED501-5 SPICE VOL. I	K-2	
☐ ED502-3 SPICE VOL. II	2-4	
☐ ED505-8 ANCHOR VOL. I	4-6	
☐ ED506-6 ANCHOR VOL. II	6-8	
☐ ED564-3 PHONICS VOL. I	K-2	
☐ ED565-1 PHONICS VOL. II	2-4	
☐ ED567-8 GRAMMAR VOL. I	4-6	
☐ ED568-6 GRAMMAR VOL. II	6-8	
☐ ED509-0 RESCUE VOL. I	K-4	
(Remedial Reading)		
☐ ED516-3 FLAIR VOL. I	3-8	
(Creative Writing)		
☐ ED527-9 DICTIONARY VOL. I	K-2	
(Single Letters)		
☐ ED528-7 DICTIONARY VOL. II	K-2	
(Blends)		
☐ ED529-5 DICTIONARY VOL. III	3-6	
☐ ED530-9 DICTIONARY VOL. IV	7-9	
☐ ED537-6 LIBRARY VOL. I	3-6	
☐ ED538-4 LIBRARY VOL. II	7-9	

MUSIC

☐ ED561-9 NOTE VOL. I	K-2
☐ ED562-7 NOTE VOL. II	3-6

ONLY $8.95 Each

EARLY LEARNING

☐ ED512-0 LAUNCH VOL. I
(Basic Readiness)
☐ ED513-9 LAUNCH VOL. II
(Additional Skills)

MATHEMATICS

☐ ED533-3 PLUS VOL. I	K-2
☐ ED534-1 PLUS VOL. II	2-4
☐ ED523-6 CHALLENGE VOL. I	4-6
☐ ED524-4 CHALLENGE VOL. II	6-8

SCIENCE

☐ ED546-5 PROBE VOL. I	K-2
☐ ED547-3 PROBE VOL. II	2-4
☐ ED550-3 INQUIRE VOL. I	4-8

SOCIAL STUDIES

☐ ED553-8 SPARK VOL. I	K-2
☐ ED554-6 SPARK VOL. II	2-4

* *

ONLY $4.50 Each

EXCLUSIVE WORD LISTS
Each book contains a graded word list — from 738 words at Level 1 to 4,325 words at Level 6.

"Work with Words" Duplicator Books Develop and Reinforce Language Skills on 6 Levels!

A creative new series from the publishers of Spice! Here's a fresh and dynamic approach to teaching and reinforcing language skills. Each master is clearly identified as to the learning objective: recognizing sounds, visual identification, word recognition, word usage, spelling, alphabetizing, word meaning, and so on. Thus the teacher can locate just the right activity at just the right time! To top if off, each book contains our exclusive and previously unpublished graded word list for that level. Each 8½ x 11" book has teacher's guide; 20 masters. Use with any basal program to extend learning through skill-building activities.

☐ ED262-8 Level 1A	738 words	☐ ED268-7 Level 4A	2970 words
☐ ED263-6 Level 1B	738 words	☐ ED269-5 Level 4B	2970 words
☐ ED264-4 Level 2A	1416 words	☐ ED270-9 Level 5A	3613 words
☐ ED265-2 Level 2B	1416 words	☐ ED271-7 Level 5B	3613 words
☐ ED266-0 Level 3A	2303 words	☐ ED272-5 Level 6A	4325 words
☐ ED267-9 Level 3B	2303 words	☐ ED273-3 Level 6B	4325 words

☐ WWP-500 Complete Set of all 12 books above $54.00
Note: "B" level books are slightly more advanced than "A" level.

Duplicators and idea-books (shown on opposite side) are available at the leading school supply dealers. Ask for them by name.
For a current catalog, contact the publisher.

IDEA-BOOKS FOR ELEMENTARY SCHOOL TEACHERS

Each book was created to meet teachers' needs for simple and explicit ideas to enrich the many subject areas presented to their students.

ONLY $8.95 Each

LANGUAGE ARTS

- ☐ ED101-X SPICE — Primary Language Arts ● Grades K-4
- ☐ ED109-5 ANCHOR — Intermediate Language Arts ● Grades 4-8
- ☐ ED128-1 RESCUE — Primary Remedial Reading ● Grades K-4
- ☐ ED112-5 FLAIR — Creative Writing ● Grades K-8
- ☐ ED122-2 SCRIBE — Handwriting ● Grades K-8
- ☐ ED126-5 PRESS — Newspaper Activities ● Grades K-8
- ☐ ED130-3 PHONICS — Primary Phonics ● Grades K-4
- ☐ ED134-6 GRAMMAR — Intermediate Grammar ● Grades 4-8
- ☐ ED131-1 LISTEN — Listening Activities ● Grades K-8
- ☐ ED133-8 VIDEO — Television Activities ● Grades K-8
- ☐ ED136-2 REFLECT — Creative Thought ● Grades 4-Adult
- ☐ ED137-0 VALUES — Values Clarification ● Grades K-8
- ☐ ED139-7 KID'S LIT — Reading Through Lit ● Grades K-8
- ☐ ED141-9 LIB. STUDIES — Library Skills ● Grades K-9

MATHEMATICS & SCIENCE

- ☐ ED103-6 PLUS — Primary Mathematics ● Grade K-4
- ☐ ED116-8 CHALLENGE — Intermediate Mathematics ● Grades 4-8
- ☐ ED118-4 METER — Metrics ● Grades K-8
- ☐ ED102-8 PROBE — Primary Science ● Grades K-4
- ☐ ED121-4 INQUIRE — Intermediate Science ● Grades 4-8
- ☐ ED140-0 NATURE — Outdoor Education ● Grades K-8

SOCIAL STUDIES

- ☐ ED104-4 SPARK — Primary Social Studies ● Grades K-4
- ☐ ED125-7 FOCUS — Intermediate Social Studies ● Grades 4-8
- ☐ ED120-6 CHOICE — Economics ● Grades K-8
- ☐ ED123-0 CAREER — Career Education ● Grades K-8
- ☐ ED135-4 COMPASS — Map Skills ● Grades K-8

SPECIALTY STUDIES

- ☐ ED111-7 LAUNCH — Preschool and Kindergarten Readiness
- ☐ ED127-3 HOLIDAY — Holiday Art ● Grades K-8
- ☐ ED105-2 CREATE — Primary Art ● Grades K-4
- ☐ ED124-9 CRAFT — Intermediate Art ● Grades 4-8
- ☐ ED113-3 NOTE — Music ● Grades K-8
- ☐ ED119-2 GROWTH — Health ● Grades K-8
- ☐ ED115-X PREVENT — Safety ● Grades K-8
- ☐ ED107-9 STAGE — Dramatics ● Grades K-8
- ☐ ED106-0 ACTION — Physical Education ● Grades K-6
- ☐ ED117-6 DISPLAY — Bulletin Board Ideas

Address: ☐ Home   ☐ School (Preferred)

Name _____

Address _____

_____

City _____ State _____ Zip _____

Idea-books and duplicators (shown on the opposite side) are available at leading school supply dealers or Educational Service, Inc., PO Box 219, Stevensville, Michigan 49127 **1-800-253-0763.**

82586